Creating a Chicana/o Red Road to Decolonization & Aztlan

Creating a Chicana/o Red Road to Decolonization & Aztlan

...a Roadmap towards a Native Identity & Worldview

YSIDRO RAMON MACIAS

By Ysidro Ramon Macias

The Compassion of the Feathered Serpent (2013)
Walking the Red Road on Chicanismo (2016)
The Domingo Martinez Paredez Mayan Reader (2017)

Cover Images/Artist

The Dreamer #1, 2014 (male)

The Dreamer #2, 2016 (female)

Both are original paintings by Malaquias Montoya. They reference the hopes and aspirations of the DACA community, the young persons brought here without legal status, who have become American. It is with those same hopes and aspirations that the Chicano seeks to navigate his way amongst American society, not for material gain, but to find an eternal and cosmic purpose.

Malaquias Montoya

malaquiasmontoya.com

Malaquias Montoya is an artistic icon of the Chicano Movement and the Chicano Artist community. He is also a master silk-screener, and his posters have reflected his political views and human emotions throughout his long career. His posters powered the Third World Liberation Front strike at UC Berkeley in early 1969. Malaquias' posters not only provided visual affirmations for numerous progressive multi-racial movements in the Bay Area during the 1960-70's, his posters also embraced the UFW movement of Cesar Chavez. His images can be found in many Movement journals, magazines, and newspapers since the 1960's. I consider him the Chicano *Jose Posada*.

Malaquias, along with his late older brother, the RCAF poet, Jose Montoya, came from a farmworker family which eventually settled in the San Joaquin Valley. Having taught his crafts at numerous universities, including Berkeley, Stanford, Notre Dame, and Texas, he is now professor emeritus at UC Davis.

Copyright © 2021 Ysidro Ramon Macias

All rights reserved

ISBN 978-1-7379953-8-8

Acknowledgment

On a cold winter night in 1980, the maestro Andres Segura arrived at my Fresno, California, home. We spent the next couple of hours catching up before he announced his visits would be less frequent. I was anxious, unsure how this news would impact my ability to absorb his worldview instruction, but he assured me he had good news. His Spirit Guides, the Seres, had instructed him to inform me, that one of their members, Coyametzli, was to be my personal Spirit Guide. Coyametzli would be always available to me to answer any questions I might have regarding the oral tradition the maestro had shared with me for eight years. I made notes of our conversation and filed them away.

Communications with the spirit world were a regular part of my upbringing within a farmworker family. Two near-death experiences, including an out-of-body event in my youth, merely confirmed the existence of the spirit world. This recognition of the spirit world, its role in our culture and daily lives, is a blessing that is hereby acknowledged. The spirit world is a real part of the Chicano experience.

Dedication

Fast forward to 2012. The maestro passed in 1997, and no one has come forward to write and preserve his native Mexica worldview. The spirit world is saying the responsibility is mine. Reviewing my old notes, the 1980 reference to Coyametzli appears. I had forgotten about Coyametzli. From that moment forward, I confidently thanked Coyametzli before every writing session, lit some copal, and the needed words flowed. This book is the fourth Coyametzli has helped me write. This book is thus appropriately dedicated to my Spirit Guide, Coyametzli.

Invocation to the Four Directions

Estrella del Oriente *

      ESTRELLA DEL ORIENTE
      QUE NOS DIO SU SANTA LUZ
      ES HORA QUE SIGAMOS
      EL CAMINO DE LA CRUZ

ORIENTE ES EL PRIMER VIENTO
QUE DEBEMOS CONQUISTAR
ES EL SÍMBOLO DEL FUEGO
QUE EN LA TRADICIÓN ESTA

PONIENTE EL SEGUNDO VIENTO
QUE DEBEMOS SALUDAR
 ES EL SIMBOLO DEL AIRE
QUE EN LA TRADICION ESTA

EL NORTE ES EL TERCER VIENTO
QUE DEBEMOS CONQUISTAR
ES EL SIMBOLO DE LA TIERRA
QUE EN LA TRADICION ESTA

EL SUR ES EL CUARTO VIENTO
QUE DEBEMOS SALUDAR
ES EL SIMBOLO DEL AGUA
QUE EN LA TRADICION ESTA

EL CENTRO ES EL QUINTO VIENTO
QUE DEBEMOS CONQUISTAR
ES EL DEL SENOR SANTIAGO
QUE EN LA TRADICION ESTA

CIELO-TIERRA, ULTIMO VIENTO
QUE DEBEMOS SALUDAR
SIMBOLOS DE PADRE Y MADRE
QUE EN LA TRADICION ESTAN

Recommended listening at start of book
*https://mediateca.inah.gob.mx/islandora_74/islandora/object/disco%3A12
(homage to the Feathered Serpent, as Venus, the Eastern morning star

Mexica Prayer

From your reddish Light cover us
From your Absolute Consciousness talk to us
From your reddish Universal Truth move us
From your Greatness, Universal Greatness, sustain our hope
so that we can drink in the source of your Knowledge
so that in company and jointly
with those Spirit/Guides of Humanity
the Spirit/Guides of the Red tradition
the Spirit/Guides of the Atlante-Tolteca tradition
the Spirit/Guides of the Teotihuacana-Teochichimeca tradition
the Spirit/Guides of the Azteca-Mexica tradition
and our own personal Spirit/Guides
so that we can fulfill our mission here on Earth
May the light and the Peace from the Giver of Life be present in our Universe,
today and always.
May the Light and the Peace from the Giver of Life be with us all
May the Light and the Peace from the Giver of Life and the spirits of the four winds
Be with us all
May the Light and the Peace from the Giver of Life and the spirit essence of the four winds
Be with us all
May the Light and the Peace of the Giver of Life and the Conquering Spirits of the four winds
Be with all of us today and always.
Everything by the will of Tonantzin Tepeyaca, our mother.

Andres Segura Granados

CONTENTS

FOREWORD

PART 1

1. Introduction 1
2. Overview of the Journey 7
3. Introduction to a Native Worldview 11
4. What is the Red Road? 27

PART TWO - THE RED ROADS

Shoshone/Bannocks 33
Preface to Shoshone/Bannock Ideology 35
1. Shoshone/Bannock Red Road 39
2. What is Indigenous Ideology? 43

The Yucatec Mayan Red Road 47
Preface to the Yucatec Mayan Red Road 49
1. Panche Be: the Search for the Roots of the Truth 55
2. Mother Nature: the Great Provider and Teacher 65
3. The Cosmic Consciousness: to Believe, Create, & Do 69
4. Chan, the Cosmic Serpents: In Lak'Ech 75

The Mexica Red Road: Esencia de las Cosas 81
Preface to the Mexica Red Road 83
1. The Law of Duality 93
2. The Law of Causation 99
3. The Law of Compensation 107

PART THREE - DECOLONIZATION

1. Do Chicanos Need to Decolonize? 113
2. Deconstructing the Spanish colonial legacy 121
3. Deconstructing the gringo colonial legacy 133

PART FOUR - AZTLAN

1. The Spiritual Aztlan 153
2. The Red Nation pueblos of Aztlan 161

PART FIVE

1. Creating a Chicano Red Road 167
2. Three Steps to Decolonization 171

Foreword

The society of the United States, despite the material comforts that it enjoys, suffers from spiritual poverty. This spiritual poverty is evidenced by the high rate of addiction in the country, a growing homelessness population, and the continual rise of mass murders and violence every year. While the media crows about the wonders of America and all it has to offer, many of its adult citizens are daily medicating themselves, while dealing with stress, depression, and other mental maladies. There is addiction to alcoholic beverages, pharmaceuticals, opioids, heroin, cocaine, methamphetamines, tobacco, cannabis, and **sugar**. We truly are a medicated society. Why?

That was a question I asked of the hippies in the Bay area in the 1960's. *"Why, given your middle- and upper-class status, and the material comforts you enjoy, are you rejecting these privileges and drugging out instead?"* Their response more often than not, was that all the materialism at their disposal was transitory and disposable. All matter was temporary. Meaning, materialism has no real meaning when you are seeking the reasons for your existence and purpose in life.

Traveling to Oaxaca and the Yucatan in 1968, I saw a poverty of materialism amongst the original pueblos of those lands, in comparison to the gringo. But that poverty of materialism was more than balanced by a passion for Life and intense religious belief, amongst an explosion of color and ceremony, that came from these same Indians. It dawned on me then, that the United States was wealthy in material comforts, but extremely poor when it came to living and appreciating Life and its blessings. In contrast, Mexico was poor in materialism, but rich and colorful in the pursuit and appreciation for Life and ceremony, and with much better food. It also raised the question in my mind, as to which had greater long-term value: materialism or spirituality?

These are the types of questions philosophy seeks to answer. If the United States truly is a medicated society, and it is, this truth reflects poverty/pain in the society. We know this poverty is not material, for we have one of the most materialistic societies on Earth. The poverty is thus obviously spiritual, reflected not only by the addictions our population pursues, but by dwindling church attendance and a growing divisive hateful environment to our politics. The addictions in this society have only grown exponentially since the 1960's. White adults are the most medicated segment of the society, addiction rampant in college dorms, cities, the suburbs, and trailer parks.

Thus, are gringo values useful, given the spiritual poverty they have generated? Can these same values help steer Chicanos to a meaningful life? Not a meaningful life measured by the amount of money you are able to acquire, but rather meaningful as in finding spiritual purpose. The answer is a resounding NO. The gringo values have had hundreds of years to prove their value, and the result is spiritual poverty. This same spiritual poverty in our country is responsible for the various addictions and mental instabilities of the population. It is also responsible for the promotion and acceptance of the Big Lie.

Conveniently, we blame Mexico and others for providing some of our addictions. But the largest and most harmful providers are home-grown:the pharmaceuticals, alcohol, opioids, methamphetamines, tobacco, and the sugar in our foods. We shall examine the growth and evolution of this spiritual poverty, its origins and history, in the building of the nation. As we shall see while deconstructing the gringo legacy, that same spiritual poverty today is energizing supporters of white supremacy, who are fearful of losing the privileges they have historically enjoyed.

Fortunately, however, Life expresses itself in Duality, and extremes on either side are always eventually balanced towards harmony. That is the natural flow of the Universe. The dual side of negative gringo values is the positive gringo value of Democracy. How long it takes harmony to manifest itself depends on either evolution, or the movement of energy humans initiate by organized protest. Since Life runs on Universal time, evolution, while inevitable, is ponderously slow.

The human energy creating the harmony of Democracy is being provided by a growing democratic tendency amongst white women and college educated whites. These portions of the white population, together with the growth of the various non-white populations, are what is driving democracy in this country to balance the white supremacy message of the Republicans.

In United States schools, we are educated to believe that philosophy was the leisure activity of Socrates, Plato, and the rest of the toga-wearing Greeks and Romans. Presumably, they borrowed some ideas and concepts from the Egyptians and, to a lesser extent, from the early Middle East civilizations. Some schools may employ a wider net of philosophy, by discussing thought from China, Japan, and India. But there is a Black Hole of Knowledge when it comes to the philosophies of the original pueblos of Abya Yala, the Americas. There is a black hole in this area because Native Thought in the Americas was never seriously considered by either the Spaniard or the European colonizers of the United States. Native Thought was never seriously considered because the European in both countries was convinced that the European had a superior culture and worldview. In their minds, why waste any time making any meaningful attempt to understand the nature-loving pagan philosophy of the conquered original pueblos?

The philosophies of Abya Yala before the coming of the European were singular, yet collective, and are expressed here as the Red Road. They were singular insofar as each pueblo had their own version of a nature-based worldview. They were collective, since all versions consistently had the same components recognizing the role of the human within the harmony of Mother Nature, and the worship of the Great Spirit. The Red Nations philosopher rarely theorized; instead, they used the science of nature and mathematics/experience to confirm their beliefs.

In many respects, the philosophy/worldview of the Red Nations was superior to, or at least equal to, any other society on Earth. If one of the prime roles of philosophy is to reflect the aspirational goals of a society, consider the **thousands of years** Red Nations pueblos lived in relative harmony, not only with each other, but with the natural world that surrounded them. Compare this harmony to the historical warfare in Europe during these same years with the Egyptians, Romans, Vikings, Germanic tribes, and warfare from Asia: Mongols, Huns, Tartars; the warring states of China and Japan.

Until recently, history in both Mexico and the United States has made knowledge of such native philosophies difficult to access or understand. The versions by the Spaniards following *la Conquista*, and their academic proponents to the current day, don't qualify as realistic narratives of the original pueblos' philosophy. The easiest way to identify a "European version," is their promotion that the Mexica had multiple gods, and that somehow Quetzalcoatl, the Feathered Serpent, was either/both a "god," and/or a human being. Professors from Harvard to Oxford to the Sorbonne have fallen victim to these Spanish-based misunderstandings and promoted them as the truth for the last 500 years.

Yet, despite this European and academic ignorance, our original pueblo ancestors did indeed have philosophers. Typically, the native philosopher was a warrior at the same time, rather than a lounger sipping *octli* while speculating about the stars. Their version of philosophy was to rigorously ponder the many questions they faced in order to exist within their environment, and to spend the time necessary for the truths to be established.

Part of their philosophy required disciplining their mental and physical capabilities, so that they could cope with the demands/expenditure of energy their investigations generated. They were master shamans, utilizing the dream world and communicating with the spirit world, all while interacting with the energy world around them. They were constantly searching for answers to the two most important questions a philosopher engages in: understanding "what is," and projecting "what can be."

Their view of Existence was very different than the view of the European. Whereas the Greek and Roman tended to use speculation to answer their philosophical questions, the original pueblo shamans avoided speculation. Instead, they were disciplined warrior scientists, studying the science of nature that they grasped through observation and interaction with their environment. They then extrapolated these findings of the science of nature on Earth, to the cosmos, in order to achieve understanding of, and integration with, the cosmos. The Red Nations philosopher thus pondered her/his existence/role, within the entire environment of the Cosmos, the sky above them, not just Mother Earth.

This book thus seeks to fill part of the black hole that exists when considering Native Thought, its roots and use, within the culture of the Red Nations. That black hole was created by the actions and writings of the Spaniards after 1519. That same black hole was also created in the United States, due to the actions of the gringo. We will put a *"tapon"* (plug) into that black hole, because the presentation of three native worldviews will demonstrate the depth and scope of the Universal vision employed by *nuestros antepasados filosofos* (our native philosophers).

Chicanos cannot rely on the school systems to finally teach the truth about the history of our country, much less the truth about our native ancestors. The schools CHOOSE not to teach true history, but they cannot teach about our native ancestors simply because the schools don't know native culture; much less know how Thought evolved, and was used, within native cultures. Chicanos thus must unearth and promote their own history and imbue this history with the oral tradition we have been blessed to receive, from our ancestors and the spirit world. Chicanos need not lead a Life limited to a materialistic European vision of reality. We just need to use all our cultural tools, including the spirit world, to discover the answers we seek.

Part One

Nothing in this world is a gift
Whatever has to be learned must be
learned the hard way...

...don Juan
Yaqui

1

Introduction

Creating a Chicana/o Red Road to Decolonization and Aztlan. Until recently, the thought that Chicanos could create their own Red Road was largely unthinkable. The reason this possibility was unthinkable was because Chicanos, like most mestizos, had historically considered their existence as being necessarily tied to Europe. That orientation has changed dramatically in the last several decades. More and more Chicanos are now expressing a native identity, while seeking more knowledge about their native ancestry.

This book is thus meant to serve as a roadmap towards a native worldview for the Chicana/o mestizo. A native roadmap with the potential to decolonize yourself from the legacy of the European, and to begin a more meaningful/focused cosmic life. The Chicano mestizo is specifically addressed, for our full-blood Chicano brothers and sisters need no introduction to the Red Road, they have been on it since birth. To create a Chicano Red Road, the mestizo necessarily has to identify as Chicano in the first place. We acknowledge that the Chicano shares significant similarities with Mexican Americans and other Mexican identities. And, like folks everywhere, Mexicans in the United States have very diverse political and identity opinions.

Some of us are naturally conservative, some moderate, some progressive, and many don't place much thought on these issues or politics. Some want to be American and may not acknowledge their

Mexican heritage. Others acknowledge being Mexican, but their individual identity is more important. Some are Mexican traditionalists who hate the name Chicano. Some prefer to identify with the wider umbrellas of Latino or Latinx. This book is not aimed at these persons. It is specifically aimed at those Raza who identify with the *conciencia* (consciousness) of Chicano or are considering doing so.

Since the roots of Chicano come from Mexico, the role of mestizos within Mexican society will be examined as we progress towards decolonization. What mestizos share, regardless of the country of their origin, or the identity they choose, is that they have roots from at least two continents. Many mestizos also have roots in Mother Africa. Some of these roots are from the foreign European, while the other roots, usually the maternal ones, are from the original pueblos. Because consideration of these native roots has historically been discouraged, **our emphasis will be on those native roots**.

Because the European colonized the Americas, what the mestizo has learned in the schools of the United States has been ONLY the European version of history. The same is true in Mexico, where the only language of instruction is the foreign Spanish. Until recently, history in both countries was studied only through European eyes. Only with the introduction of Ethnic Studies in the 1970's, did the mestizo in the United States get to consider some of her/his native roots. Over the succeeding decades, more young Chicanos have begun to explore their native selves. The growth of native consciousness is currently being expressed by the thousands of *danza Azteca* groups that have joined the sacred circle throughout the Southwest, and beyond, in recent years.

This native consciousness is also being expressed by Chicanos in the academic community, where teaching/examining the history and culture of the original pueblos is being studied. The growth of this native consciousness is an antidote to the spiritual poverty that colonized life has given the Mexican in the United States. If the society you live in isn't providing you with the spiritual nourishment that you need, and it isn't, then **why not consider a native perspective**, especially since it is part of your heritage?

To continue building a bridge between the Chicano and his native roots, this book will present elementary information on the belief systems of our Native American relatives and Mexican ancestors. These belief systems are all versions of what is known as the Red Road. The belief systems presented are evidence that Thought has long been an exercise of the native mind. This tradition of Thought, generated by an intense relationship with Mother Nature and the cosmos, is spiritual nourishment of another kind. A spiritual nourishment that comes from your gut, a spiritual nourishment that can light the path of your life.

After the introductory material, the book begins by presenting three different versions of the Red Road. It then explores the issue of decolonization. In our case, specifically the decolonization from both the Spanish legacy of Mexico and the gringo in the United States. It explains how decolonizing yourself will allow you the freedom and clarity to travel on the Red Road. It will then get philosophical and describe the possible afterlife destination of the *spiritual Aztlan*. It will explain why you are empowered as a member of the mestizo Nation of Aztlan to create your own Red Road. The book will finish by providing an outline for you to create and travel on your own Chicano Red Road.

To aid us in the first step, three native worldviews will be presented. The first of these is Native American, that of the Shoshone/Bannocks of the western United States. Interestingly, the oral tradition of the Shoshone/Bannocks contains Aztec roots. The other two native worldviews presented are from Mexico: the Yucatec Mayan and the Aztec/Mexica of central Mexico.

Since the goal is to understand and create a Chicano Red Road, let's start with the definition/identity of Chicano. There are a multitude of opinions as to the origins/meaning of "Chicano." I can only relay my experiences since my birth in 1944. I grew up in the Salinas Valley, where the older Mexicans identified with being Mexican, while the youth chose the identity of being Chicano. Of course, our female halves identified with Chicana. For us, being Chicano meant we were Mexicans born or raised in the United States. Being Chicano thus was a cultural identification, with no politics attached to the name. This was always my identity from youth through my Army years ending in 1965.

On May 13, 1967, Chicano high-school and college students from throughout mostly southern California gathered at Loyola University near the Los Angeles airport. Being a student at Santa Monica City College, I attended as well. This meeting was the first where large numbers of Raza students gathered at a conference and represents the start of what became known as the Chicano Movement. UMAS for southern California Chicanos, and MASC for northern Califas Chicanos, were the student group names that emerged from Loyola.

At this meeting, we re-defined what Chicano meant. It transformed into both a political as well as a cultural identity. Within this new political identity, came a personal commitment to work on behalf of the Chicano/Mexican community. The political identity also rejected white America's "lift yourself by your bootstraps" lie as well as the "American dream" winner-take-all goal. These gringo goals were rejected because history had shown that they didn't apply to Mexicans. The political identity further placed the value of Mexican culture above all things white American.

In the succeeding decades, the growth of interest in our native *antepasados* has caused a revelation of the extensive native components of the Chicano identity. This expansion of the definition of Chicano goes beyond the political identity adopted at Loyola. Chicano (Xikano) was shown to be derived from the Nahuatl pronunciation for mexicano (Meshicano). To the full blood of Mexico, who instead identifies with his/her pueblo, a Meshicano essentially refers to a mestizo, or a Westernized native. Both Chicano and Meshicano were shown to have linguistically evolved from Mexica (Meshica), the Aztec founding pueblo of Tenochtitlan.

After the birth of Mexico in 1821, its citizens became, in Nahuatl, Meshicanos. The belief is that Nahuatl-speaking immigrants, once in the United States, referred to the Mexican mestizos already here as "Meshicanos." In time, the "Me" was linguistically dropped, resulting in "Chicano."

The cosmic implications of Mexica/Meshicano/Chicano were revealed when the Mayan maestro Domingo Martinez Paredez recited the origins of the name Mexica. Mexica was revealed to be the Nahuatl interpretation of the name given them by the Yucatec Mayans, that name being **Meexikanoob**. The Mayans gave the visiting Aztec clans the name **Meexikanoob** because of the feathers they wore glued to their faces, which showed their reverence for the Feathered Serpent.

In Mayan, **Meexikanoob** means "Bearded Serpents with Feathers." Thus, **Meexikanoob** metaphorically meant "those who follow the Feathered Serpent." Because the Feathered Serpent is the exoteric representative of the Great Spirit, you could say that Mexica really means "those who worship the Great Spirit." Even though most Chicanos are unaware of the true meaning of their identity, that of being "one who follows the Feathered Serpent," that is the historical and linguistic definition of Mexica; and thus, Chicano.

I personally observe an even wider definition of Chicano, which I call the "Malcolm X addendum." Malcolm X was an inspirational leader who grew up hating white people. When he visited Mecca, his consciousness expanded. It expanded because he realized that the color of one's skin was irrelevant when it came to worshipping Allah. I too, grew up hating white people, before learning the lesson of Tolerance within a native worldview. My life experiences in political activism have shown that being "Chicano," is a matter of consciousness. Many Latinos, and some whites, identified with being Chicano during these times. Based on their consciousness and actions, I consider them Chicanos as well.

That is the definition of Chicano that I observe and practice. A Chicano who honors, daily gives thanks to, and has faith in the Great Spirit. I follow the Great Spirit by daily being thankful for living a lifetime. I follow/worship the Great Spirit by practicing harmony and balance with all my relatives, while constantly giving thanks to the Great Spirit throughout every day. I follow and believe in the Great Spirit, and only the Great Spirit. I do not require prophets/saints/popes/bishops/reverends, priests, nuns, or monks, to speak with, and have an interactive relationship with, the Great Spirit. Of course, as a Chicano, my community is always foremost in my thoughts and hopes. That is essentially the Chicano Red Road that I travel on.

2

Overview of the Journey

The Red Road is a common-sense approach to viewing and interacting with Life. The foundation of any Red Road is worshipping the Great Spirit and recognizing Mother Earth and all her organisms/forms, including humans, as equal and harmonious cooperators in the unfolding of Life. Every Red Road is personal to the human, since we are eternal spirits experiencing our own unique human lifetime and will make those choices which our eternal spirit (the unconscious mind) advises, are for our greater good. Assuming the reader is a Chicana/o/x, the Red Road you will create will be a Chicana/o/x Red Road. If your identity is other than Chicano, then create your own Red Road around your own culture. The Red Road is wide enough to allow Black, Yellow, and White travelers. At the end of the day, we are all humans. To aid you in this task, three native worldviews follow.

These native worldviews will allow you to understand the vision they project, and their common-sense approach to incorporate oneself with one's environment. They will demonstrate the depth and width of their worldview, a worldview concerned with integrating the human of the Red Nations beyond Mother Earth all the way to the cosmos. The factors and methodology that led to the creation of these worldviews will be self-evident. They will demonstrate that the Red Road is a scientific road, which utilizes lessons from Mother Nature to attain harmony, tolerance, and integration. A scientific road established over centuries of observation and interaction by our disciplined ancestors with the Life around them.

The first native worldview is that of the Shoshone/Bannocks of modern Idaho and surrounding states. The second worldview is the Yucatec Mayan, taken from the writings of Domingo Martinez Paredez. The third worldview is the Mexica, taught to me by Andres Segura Granados, the Azteca/Mexica *capitan-general de concheros*, of Mexico-Tenochtitlan. These will be preceded by a recitation of my personal introduction into a native worldview.

After you have had an opportunity to absorb all three native worldviews, the next step the book takes is to consider the need for Decolonization. In order to weigh the importance of, and need to, decolonize, the initial question of whether Chicanos/Mexicans are colonized will be examined. Because Chicanos are Mexicans, any decolonization process requires an analysis of the societies mestizos have lived under since 1519.

This starts with the Spanish white supremacy and privilege racial system the Spaniards imposed on their colony of New Spain until 1821. The second colonial status that needs to be examined for possible deconstruction is the United States history of white supremacy and privilege, which was built upon the foundation of Calvinism. By having first read and absorbed the three native worldviews, the possible needed deconstruction of both colonial (Spanish and gringo) legacies will become much clearer.

With the evolution of consciousness, having absorbed the information given, and considered decolonization; you will be ready to consider Aztlan, the possible final destination of the Chicano Red Road. It is not the physical Aztlan, wherever that may have been located, of Aztec oral tradition. This destination is necessarily a *spiritual Aztlan*. How can we find this spiritual Aztlan? While the Red Road is a forward-looking cyclical worldview, its roots are to be found in our *antepasados* (native ancestors).

That is why we shall examine the three native worldviews presented in this book: to understand our roots better, and to recognize the tree of descendants these roots were meant to sustain. As the Chicano Red Road evolves forward on the circle of Life, it will cyclically take our spirits to where they began their journey: **Tamoanchan**. The Chicano Red Road thus can be our vehicle to continue our journey as eternal spirits experiencing a unique human lifetime. When that Chicano/a spirit arrives in Aztlan, it will have found its **Tamoanchan**. There, it will continue the process of spiritual transformation which will lead to the next human lifetime. These were part of the teachings of the maestro Andres Segura Granados.

After these steps, the reader will be ready to build. They are empowered to do so as members of the mestizo Nation of Aztlan, which is part of the Red Nations. For those readers ready to travel on the Chicano Red Road, they can begin the construction and visualization of their own version of the Red Road.

Traveling on the Red Road requires developing the consciousness to integrate yourself with the environment which surrounds you daily. Traveling on the Red Road is not complicated, it is essentially based on following/practicing common sense and having respect for all forms of Life. The Red Road describes the interactive relationship with the Great Spirit that you develop, as you meet and experience the challenges of life.

For those Chicanos who have always honored their Mexican culture, building your Chicano Red Road will be second nature. There are two critical components to any Red Road: 1) worship the Great Spirit, and 2) honor and respect Mother Earth. These components teach that all Life is the Great Spirit, and all organisms of Life on Mother Earth, including humans, are her children, and equal to each other. The other components of any Red Road are common sense beliefs most Mexicans already practice.

For the purposes of this book, mestizo is synonymous with Chicano/a/x. "Chicano" automatically includes Chicanas and Chicanx, and any other variation of "Chicano." Chicano can be spelled Xicano or Xikano as well. While Mexican Americans and those from Mexico and Latin America can also be mestizo; unless they are specifically mentioned in this book, the word mestizo is synonymous with the Chicano identity. Mother Earth and Mother Nature are synonymous with each other. Native/original pueblo/Indian are synonymous with each other. Nahuatl became the language of the Aztecs/Mexicas, and pueblos of that linguistic culture, the Nahuas, are synonymous with Aztec/Mexica. The *spiritual Aztlan* is synonymous with **Tamoanchan**, and the Native American "Happy Hunting Ground." There are multiple names for the Absolute Being. The Great Spirit, Ometeotl, God, Dios, Wakan Tanka, amongst others, are ALL the same and only Absolute Being.

To state that the Feathered Serpent was the exoteric representative of the Great Spirit, is to understand that the Feathered Serpent was commonly seen and understood by the people of the original pueblos, to be the same as the Great Spirit. The Feathered Serpent thus served as the material symbol of the Great Spirit, which otherwise is pure Energy and has no image. An analogy can be made to Jesus, who serves in the mind of many Christians, to be the same as God.

3

Introduction to a Native Worldview

I was raised by my 1890's born paternal grandparents, who were both *campesinos* from the mountains of Jalisco. My grandfather came first, during the Mexican Revolution, seeking work in the orchards of Orange County, California. Other farmworkers from his small village in the Jalisco mountains were already there picking oranges, so it was logical for him to go there as well. Four years and four kids later, my grandmother followed him to Orange County in 1922. Eventually, the family grew to 14 children, while they migrated to the Salinas Valley. Years later, after having lived in a tent encampment close to the town cemetery, they managed to buy property in Soledad, California. It was in Soledad where I grew up in their household; since my father, their oldest son, was killed at the age of 28.

Like most of the Mexican kids in Chole (Soledad), I worked summers in the vegetable fields of the Valley from elementary school until leaving before my last year of high school. I purposely mention my farmworker background, because as Bonfil Batalla cites in his important book, *"Mexico Profundo,"* there is very little distinction between the *campesino* mestizo and the natives of the original pueblos of Mexico. Not only does the *campesino* mestizo likely share a large percentage of native blood, more importantly, the living conditions/culture of both the *campesino* mestizo and the original pueblo native are very similar. They are very similar because both communities are tied to and work with Mother Earth for their existence. They are also very similar because the campesino mestizo is likely to have retained much of his native culture, beliefs, and manner of interaction with life.

Four years after both grandparents passed away, I moved to Long Beach to live with my mother and finish my final year of high school. This gave me the opportunity to taste/experience the life of a city Chicano and compare this existence to my rural Chicano roots. What I saw amongst the city Chicanos was an alienation from Mother Earth, leading to a poverty of the mind, and a willingness to kill other Chicanos for nothing. In the *campo*, by contrast, the rural Chicano was poorer in money and comforts, but much richer in living a life tied to Mother Earth, all while interacting with people and observing life and ceremonies around them more intensely. Rural Chicanos also took the time to talk to each other, and settled most disputes with *chingasos* (punches), rather than bullets.

Coming from a *campesino* background in this country is the closest a Chicano will get to live and understand a native rhythm, if not a worldview. At my late age comes a recognition that I was blessed to have been born into and raised within a farmworker family. With that background came close ties to Mother Earth, and an ability to experience a meaningful life without emphasis on material goods. As long as we had room to run, and we did, having open fields, railroad tracks, and rivers; and beans, potatoes, tortillas, chile, and fideo to eat; that was a smorgasbord of food and exploration for us. I never felt poor growing up in that environment. This rural upbringing also made me more receptive to the teachings of the maestro.

In 1968, when I became interested in learning more about my Mexican native ancestors, most of the literature available on the subject of pre-1519 Mexican history had been written by Europeans and their descendants. These descendants were the entire academic world of Europe and the United States, and included Mexican authors like Angel Garibay, Alfonso Caso, and Miguel Leon-Portilla, then considered the *"pesados"* (heavyweights) of Aztec studies.

These European literary versions painted a picture of an empire-hungry Aztec/Mexica society, with mass bloody human-heart sacrificial ceremonies dripping down temple stairs, where multiple strange-looking gods were worshipped. To top it all off, according to the Spaniards, the natives were practicing the most primitive and "non-philosophical" of all religions: a pagan nature-worshipping worldview. All the European versions of their conquest thus justified it as fulfilling the "need for Christian religion and civilization."

That was the reality with regards to available literature in English on ancient Mexican history in 1968. Otherwise, my poor Spanish-reading skills were tested with the numerous Mexican texts published by the UNAM; all long and ponderous. For the rare native Mexican perspective in English, the translated *Popol Vuh* was available, as well as interpretations of the *Books of Chilam Balam*. Both were written in the 1600-1700's by Mayans using a newly-learned Latin alphabet, and both employed a heavy use of metaphors to hide their true content. These books thus are riddles, unless the reader is familiar with Mayan metaphors.

Being mestizo, literature was the only vehicle I had to learn from, since I had no access to any native community in either Mexico or the United States in the late 1960's. Thus, seeking a native perspective on our ancestors was challenging, considering that 99% of all books written on them promoted the European versions. These European versions didn't contain the discussions I was seeking, which was to understand how my native ancestors defined God, visualized Life, the Universe, and their other religious beliefs. I wanted to understand how the original pueblos worldviews compared to the Catholic faith I had been raised under. I wanted more answers than the Catholic priests either knew or were willing to share. This questioning, seeking nature, went back to my early youth.

My grandmother who raised me was an extreme Catholic. She was a *campesina* her entire life, working the fields until her death at 61, while giving birth to and raising 14 children. Most often she worked with the *cortito*, the short-handle hoe spacing lettuce seedlings while bent over ten hours a day. She recited multiple rosaries all day long, as she worked the rows Monday through Saturday. In the evenings, before going to bed, she would lead a round of rosaries with my aunts for another hour or two. She demanded and expected that all her children and eventually 36 grandchildren, live their lives around the Catholic calendar throughout the year. That is why I say she was an extreme Catholic.

The other half of my grandparent Duality was my angry grandfather. He was angry for many reasons, including that his health was poor having labored as a *campesino* his entire life, and he was extremely resentful of the racism he had faced from the gabacho. He had no love for the hypocrisy and racism of the Church as well, criticizing the Irish priests for their fawning behavior towards the landowners, the Italian-Swiss. He insisted that only Spanish be spoken in our home, adding scornfully that English *"es la lengua de los perros!"* (is the language of dogs!). This combination of being raised by an extreme Catholic grandmother, and society-schooled by an aware and angry grandfather, made me question racism in our society, as well as the practice of the Catholic religion. This questioning nature continued throughout my elementary and high school years, and after enlisting in the Army upon high school graduation.

Before my discharge from the Army three years later, I embarked on a self-taught instruction of the world's religions for close to a year. I was stationed in the Arizona desert with plenty of time to think. The main religions like Hinduism, Buddhism, Islam, and Judaism were considered, and somewhat understood, but others like Confucianism, Zoroastrianism, and Shinto were also considered. I was seeking answers to many questions and was hopeful of finding answers to these questions.

I went into my self-study with an open mind regarding those religions I was studying. Had I found the answers I sought in another religion, I would have converted to that religion. Though there were attractive features to be found in all the religions studied, my conclusion one year later was that none of them offered any more answers than the few the Catholic religion already offered. This led to my leaving the Catholic faith, not having found any intuitive answers to my questions.

That was my religious background and experience until seven years later, in 1972, upon meeting the maestro Andres Segura Granados. We were at the TENAZ Festival, conversing after just having met, and spontaneously the maestro began revealing his native worldview. Instinctively in my mind, everything he said was logical, made sense, and connected with me as something that was part of my DNA. At the same time, I could see a wide ray of spiritual sunlight shining down upon our conversation. Multiple answers intuitively came flooding into my consciousness from that first encounter. My gut told me that I had found my philosophical home, and the meaning to my life that I had been seeking, was coming. I trusted then that my future would confidently reveal more answers from this native worldview of *La Esencia de las Cosas*. But I'm getting ahead of my story.

Returning to 1968, I was in the beginning stages of my search for meaning to my life. In this beginning stage, I relied on Native American books written by native authors, to try to grasp the beliefs of an original pueblo worldview. Thus, my self-education into my ancestors was limited to what I could derive from these Native American books. Those books spoke of a Native American culture with beliefs like my own Mexican one, and their pictures confirmed that the Lakota or Hopi face depicted could easily be Mexican. The books and pictures confirmed that we were the same people. Before this revelation of being "native," I had always looked towards Europe for answers to any questions I had.

But the spiritual and religious practices didn't match up, when comparing the Native American worldviews to what the Europeans wrote about the Mexican original pueblos. Native Americans weren't into mass human sacrifice, and they only worshipped the Great Spirit, not the multiple gods the Aztecs supposedly had. Intuitively, I knew something was wrong, but where could I get the answers I was seeking? Over time, these repetitive questions became like focused prayers to the Great Spirit, asking for more clarity.

As I delved deeper and deeper into grasping a native worldview, primarily from the Native Americans, my hunger for more information grew. At the same time, I shared my growing information/awareness in this area by teaching courses on Mexican indigenous philosophy at Berkeley, Merritt College, and Santa Clara University. I wanted to share the information I had in the hopes of generating discussion with other Chicanos. But the texts for the courses I taught were based on the available books on the subject; and again, outside of the *Popol Vuh*, all other books promoted the "European versions." I needed reliable native sources, preferably from Mexico, to balance my instruction and make it more native; and thus, objective in its presentation.

In 1972, the Great Spirit answered my prayers for more knowledge in this area when I met the maestro Andres Segura Granados at the Teatro Nacional de Aztlan (TENAZ) Festival held that year at Orange Coast College in Costa Mesa, California. Present at the TENAZ festival were Chicano theater groups from throughout the Southwest, including my own from Santa Clara University. The maestro was the guest choreographer for an invited Mexican student group from Cuernavaca. The Universe answered my prayers because in the maestro, what I had lacked before regarding my native ancestors, which was a credible source to learn from, suddenly appeared with many more answers than I had questions.

I was then an academic Chicano with a master's degree from Berkeley, and a professor at the Jesuit Santa Clara University. Even though my background in the Chicano Movement since 1967 was that of radical cultural nationalist; having organized multiple Chicano community and college groups, including a Brown Beret chapter; was co-Chairman of the TWLF at Berkeley; worked for the Cuban Revolution at *La Isla de Juventud*; my belief system was totally Western in its orientation. My childhood Catholic faith still defined what I generally thought of life, the Universe, and God, even though I had left the Church in 1965. I still defined reality through Western philosophy and beliefs, even after my political involvement had flushed away the "American dream," and confirmed the deep white racism and privilege that drives everything in United States society.

Yet, even during my "revolutionary years" of the early *movimiento* (1967-72), I had never lost faith in, and belief in, God. But I kept this faith and belief private, since many of my contemporary activist Chicanos were becoming critical of religion or flirting with atheism. When the maestro introduced me to Ometeotl, I felt I "could come out of the closet," in regards my belief and faith in God. Within his native worldview, it was okay and common to express your love and belief in the Great Spirit on a daily multiple basis. Many conversations began and ended with *"El es Dios!"*

The Great Spirit the maestro introduced as Ometeotl was the Universal Life Force of pure Energy. He described this Energy in a way so I could understand that the Universe had a definable structure, and a recognizable flow to Life, even though it continuously evolves. In the Nahua worldview, the continuing evolution of Ometeotl, required Laws to govern this recognizable structure and flow of Existence. Ometeotl observes/honors these same Laws for there to be consistency throughout Existence.

The worldview the maestro painted recognized a rhythm to Life, had been derived over centuries of observation with Nature and interaction with the spirit world, and resulted in a cosmic purpose for a human lifetime. His explanation of the evolution of Ometeotl into diverse material bodies and spiritual energy was like being exposed to a world library of knowledge, compared to the one-line sentence Catholics use to describe God: *"God is, God has always been, God will always be."* Fin. Finito. Todo. That's all folks.

Eating at the Catholic table of knowledge had been like having a one-taco plate. A mini taco at that. In comparison, the native worldview the maestro presented was a smorgasbord of choices, all interacting with each other and guaranteed to please your palate. His worldview guaranteed to please your palate because the meal was harmonious and balanced, while making you, as the diner, part of the dining experience.

When the maestro introduced Ometeotl to me outside the college cafeteria at Costa Mesa, the most pressing questions I had for him was to explain the multiple gods and human sacrifice of the Mexica. The existence and multiplicity of these gods and mass sacrifice was something totally different from anything I had read about in Native American books. Yet the Mexica and other Mexican pueblos were also part of the Red Nations. *How could they have corrupted/distorted their worldviews so differently, that human sacrifice was a common occurrence and multiple gods were present everywhere?*

Furthermore, according to the Western academics, Ometeotl was seemingly competing with Huitzilopochtli, Quetzalcoatl, Coatlicue, and multiple other gods on the ceremonial calendar. What I had never considered in reading these Western/European versions was the possibility that what the Spanish wrote about our ancestors was FALSE. Or, if not outright false, based on a gross misunderstanding of the native worldviews before them. The possibility that someone could challenge the veracity of the European versions had never entered my mind.

After all, those Spanish versions were mostly written in the 1500's, during and soon after *la Conquista*; and provide the academic foundation for the anthropology approach to the original pueblos. Anthropology as in "their history/culture is dead and buried, and only their bones are of interest." These are the texts in the millions which occupy libraries the world over. Academics the world over have taken these Spanish versions as gospel truth, and then proceeded to use them to state their opinions and conclusions, in one book after another, for the last 500 years.

The maestro laughed at my anguish and immediately flushed the Spanish versions away. *"Son falsos"* (they're false), he cackled. He explained that the falsity of the Spanish versions wasn't so much what they documented about existing Indian life in Mexico at the time of the Conquest. Their Falsity was painting the so-called native religious and philosophical beliefs as they did: human sacrifice with bloody hearts on temple stairs and multiple gods galore. A Falsity based both on misunderstanding the native philosophical beliefs grounded in the science of nature, and the desire to demonize those beliefs by inventing non-existent ceremonies.

What the Spaniards didn't tell their readers, was that they NEVER witnessed, any of these so-called practices of the Mexica. They purposely created narratives involving mass sacrifice and multiple gods in order to justify the forced conversion of the natives to their foreign religion. Another historical example of a Big Lie, and, in this case, its 500-year impact. The native sources for the purported mass sacrifices were not the *tlamatinime*, the "learned ones," who really knew the accumulated knowledge of their pueblo. Instead, they were natives available for hire or more likely, intimidated into cooperating. The European belief that multiple gods existed, was a gross misunderstanding of the role of the spirit world interwoven with Mother Nature, in the native mind.

The maestro explained that like all advanced societies, the Mexica had individuals whose role was to preserve and maintain the religious and philosophical knowledge of their pueblo. These were the individuals who were known as the *tlamatinime*. Most of the *tlamatinime* were killed by the conquistadores or priests, and those who survived hid in order to survive. They were not about to share their knowledge with the Spanish priests. Not having any native sources who truly knew the knowledge of the original pueblos, the Spaniards utilized those surviving natives willing to tell them essentially what they wanted to hear. What they wanted to hear was the ability to paint a picture of a native religion so awful, bloody and unjust, that natives would rush to receive the baptismal waters from the Catholic priests.

In other words, the Spaniards weren't interested in the truth as scholars; their primary purpose as Catholic priests was in promoting their foreign Catholic religion upon the natives by demonizing native beliefs and threatening death. Not only demonizing and threatening from the pulpit but burning and destroying any material evidence documenting native beliefs as well. The existing codices survived despite the wholesale destruction of many native documents by the priests. There were no known "conquistador scholars" amongst the Spaniards.

The most demonized native "god" was Quetzalcoatl, for in the native mind the Feathered Serpent was the exoteric representative of the Great Spirit, and therefore, many temples and edifices were populated with the face of the Serpent. The Spaniards and their academic descendants have never understood this connection between the Feathered Serpent and the Great Spirit. Instead, they continue to push narratives that Quetzalcoatl was either/both a god and a human being, including their Jesus-wannabe, Topiltzin.

Note: Simply put, the Feathered Serpent is one of the aspects of our Father Sun. Here the Feathered Serpent represents the Great Spirit, because in the role as the Feathered Serpent, Father Sun dispenses the consciousness, the energy/spirit from the Great Spirit, to give Life to our human bodies. The Feathered Serpent is also that aspect of our Father Sun which led to integration with the cosmos, since as its children, we walk/fly in the Universe, alongside our parent. By its gift of consciousness, the Feathered Serpent allowed humans to access the Cosmic Consciousness, leading to cosmic integration. The planet Venus, the spirit of the wind-Ehecatl, amongst others; are also aspects of the Feathered Serpent.

But the natives still weren't interested in converting, despite the Spanish *mentirero* (lies) and demonization. The religion of the Spaniards didn't make any sense to the natives; to them, it was literally a cult of Jesus, a former human being. This cult worship of a former human being was totally unknown within a native worldview. Nevertheless, the Spanish priests persisted in promoting their religion by writing false renditions about native religious beliefs and forcing Indian children to be educated in the histories the Spanish wrote/invented.

Most texts were written in a form demanded by their order (Jesuits, Franciscans, Dominicans). All were written with a goal of demonizing the native beliefs and justifying the promotion of Catholicism in order to "save and civilize the pagan Indians." These false narratives about our ancestors written by the Spanish priests have become the accepted truths within Western academic communities for the last 500 years.

The first lesson the maestro imparted, thus, was the need to challenge and not believe the European versions of what constituted our native truths. ALL these versions were written from the perspective/intent of the foreign European; NONE of them were written from the perspective of a member of the original pueblos. ALL these versions were written from the perspective of justifying the "religious salvation" the Spaniard brought to his new colony.

Remember, he would remind me, the Europeans believed and promoted within their academic communities for over a thousand years that the planets and Sun rotate around the Earth, and they almost lynched Galileo for believing otherwise. They also thought the world was flat. In other words, wrong opinions and misunderstandings don't become VALID just because they've been around for 500 years, come from the dominant white culture, and fill libraries everywhere.

When I realized that NONE of the alleged ceremonies and human sacrifices of the Mexica were ever witnessed by a Spaniard, the European versions immediately became suspect. Yet, there was still the issue of the multiple polytheistic gods our ancestors allegedly believed in. The European version coffins were nailed and buried, when the maestro calmly explained that the multiple "gods" of the Mexica were, in fact, spirits. Spirits misunderstood as being "gods."

"Eran espiritus, no dioses" (they were spirits, not gods). All those being honored on a given ceremonial day, the maestro stressed, were spirits, not gods. Every part of Mother Nature has its own spirit, meaning the animal kingdom, birds, fishes, plants. Rivers, streams, brooks, clouds, rocks. They all have spirits. In fact, for the Mexica, every form of life has its own soul and spirit. Every day has its own spirit as well, the spirit of the day. Father Sun has many aspects (the Rising Sun-Huitzilopochtli, the Noonday Sun-Tonatiuh, the Sun of Rain-Tlaloc, the Feathered Serpent-Quetzalcoatl, the Smoking Mirror-Tezcatlipoca); each aspect has its own spirit. The same is true for the many aspects of Mother Earth.

Thus, when the native celebrated different spirits with dances, flowers, poems, and ceremonies, he was celebrating those aspects of Life and Mother Nature which the spirit represented. You could say the native was complementing Mother Nature for the dress she was wearing that day. Regardless, as all were spirits, all were part of Ometeotl. These celebrations with the environment and the Life it provides was part of the interactive relationship our ancestors had with the Universe/Great Spirit.

Once I grasped this vision of the Mexica worldview; that the multiple "gods," were in fact, spirits, everything I had read in Native American books on the same subject lined up the same. By this time, the purported never-witnessed mass sacrifices had been flushed from my mind. There was one, and only one, Great Spirit in the Mexica religious pantheon, the same as what Native Americans also believed.

There was, however, more specificity and philosophy in Ometeotl as the Great Spirit, than anything I had found in Native American descriptions. Then again, the Mexica were focused on the movement/science of energy. As part of that specificity and philosophy, the dual Ometeotl had three Universal Laws which She/He also obeyed. In this Duality, *Omecihuatl* is the female energy of Ometeotl, while *Ometecuhtli* is the male energy of Ometeotl.

The maestro acknowledged that *La Esencia de las Cosas* was not to be found in any book. This was part of the knowledge the ***tlamatinime*** took underground to escape Spanish notice in the 1500's. He learned some of *La Esencia de la Cosas* from his *tlamatini* (teacher) within the *conchero* tradition. But more importantly, he had primarily incorporated knowledge from his Spirit Guides, the **Seres;** to arrive at his understanding of *La Esencia de las Cosas*.

He maintained a daily communication throughout his life with *los Seres* for guidance and information. He was evasive as to this instruction, but always gave credit to his *conchero* superiors and the spirit world. He was evasive as to the **Seres** because that was a responsibility he had sworn to, as part of receiving the oral tradition from them. But he did share the following:

The spirit world he was in contact with were his Spirit Guides, which he called ***los Seres*** (literally "the Beings," though I interpreted the name as "the Seers"). Spirit Guides are as the name describes: spirits who choose to become your guide(s) and help you with tasks the Great Spirit has assigned to you. He described the **Seres** as a spiritual council whose members had been from the original pueblos in their prior lifetimes, and who had united in the spirit world after the European invasion.

The reason the *Seres* united in the spirit world, the maestro explained, was to counter the effects of the Conquest by promoting the preservation and maintenance of the native consciousness, traditions, and worldview, within the Red Nations. The *Seres* were able to accomplish these goals for hundreds of years by educating (seeding) selected spirits with specific tasks prior to their human births. The seeded spirits then had lifetimes which involved their maintaining native traditions. This responsibility and methodology would continue until such time as the native consciousness would arise again, in the Turtle continent and her sister.

The *Seres* had been somewhat successful in Mexico since *la Conquista*, because most native communities remained in their ancestral lands, while practicing syncretized Catholicism to please the local priests. Their native traditions and worldview had continued while they muttered Catholic ceremony. Even amongst the metropolis sprawl of Mexico City, the descendants of the Aztecas/Mexica maintained their beliefs within the conchero tradition. These *conchero* dancers number in the millions in central Mexico alone.

However, in the early 1970's, most of the mestizos of Mexico were a lost cause, the maestro asserted. Most of them were too interested in being European to have any interest in their native roots. But the mestizos of *el Norte* offered a unique opportunity, the maestro explained. It was the emergence of the Chicano in el Norte that had drawn the interest of the *Seres*. The *Seres* saw an opportunity to expand the native traditions and worldview amongst the Chicanos. At the same time, the *Seres* wanted to create a bridge to facilitate Chicano interaction with their Native American relatives.

The bridge to accomplish this, the *Seres* believed, would be the return of the dance circle amongst Chicanos. This potential for the growth of consciousness amongst the Chicanos, and the resultant reunification with the Native Americans, was part of the prophesy of the return of the Red Nations, the maestro asserted. This was also the reason the *Seres* had directed him to go North and start spreading the seeds of *indigenismo*.

*NOTE: the dance circle has indeed returned amongst Chicanos and continues to grow every year. There are now thousands of Chicano and Mexican danza Azteca groups in the country. Some follow the conchero tradition, others are less ceremonial and traditional. Some are **centroamericanos**. Every year their children are likely to become danzantes as well.*

That's what he was doing being the choreographer for los *Mascarones*, a Mexican student theater group from Cuernavaca, at the 1972 TENAZ festival in Costa Mesa. Even though the choreography he employed for them was all ballet-style European movements, and not danza; for him, this was an opportunity to check the Chicanos out. **Would his seeds take root here?** As events would play out shortly, this introduction to the *chicanada* would thereafter consume a large part of his life. Even when his stature grew within the *conchero* community when he was named *capitan-general de la danza*, the highest title achievable amongst the Aztec dancers of central Mexico, he remained focused on both his danza group Xinaxtli and his activities in *el Norte*.

These activities became numerous after he came to teach and help my *teatro* group during two quarters at UC Irvine in 1973. Lectures at colleges throughout the Southwest and elsewhere followed for years thereafter; long question and answer sessions into the night with Raza youth everywhere; helping to start multiple Chicano *danza* groups throughout the Southwest; constant movement throughout every day and extensive travel made possible with 20-minute power naps and coffee loaded halfway with sugar and accompanied with the sweetest of pastry; all juiced up, the maestro moved everywhere and at all times in a fast walk. He never assumed he would be alive the following day.

Before many knew it, he had made contacts with and was visiting the Hopi and Navajo in Arizona; dancing with the Lakotas in the Dakotas; sharing cornbread with the Lagunas in New Mexico, Crows in Montana, and multiple other pueblos throughout this country. He even journeyed to connect with the Iroquois Nations in New York and the First Nations community of Canada. He was always spreading the seeds of *indigenismo* as directed by the **Seres** and creating a bridge between the Native American pueblos and Chicanos. This would continue to be his life until 1997 when, gathering with a group of Chicanos, they re-enacted the believed Aztlan journey from New Mexico and walked all the way to Mexico City/Tenochtitlan. On that march, he contracted a disease, and shortly journeyed to his *Tamoanchan* at age 66.

This is a good opportunity to state what should be obvious: the Mexica worldview contained within this book is my recollection and understanding of the maestro's *La Esencia de las Cosas* worldview. Meaning, this is limited to that material I was able to digest, understand, and retain over a 40-year period. I have unfortunately forgotten a wealth of knowledge he imparted. Fortunately, there are some older YouTube videos where you can see and hear the maestro at various stages in his life, and at different locations. The maestro had much more to share and enlighten us on, and these videos help to amplify those contributions.

"La palabra de los ancianos." Part one has the maestro explaining the human organic integration of our Father Sun's energy when greeting the *Jefito* every morning. Part two centers on the integration of all living beings as medicine for ourselves. Both are in Spanish with musical background and the maestro speaking in true *tlamatini* voice.

A one-hour presentation of the maestro is titled "Andres Segura Granados. Conferencia." This again is in Spanish.

Much more interesting is a five-part video entitled "El es Dios INAH 1965." This is an extensive documentary by Mexican filmmakers in the middle 1960's. It features the maestro in his younger days when he had recently become a *conchero*. The filmmakers were interested in understanding and documenting the *conchero* community of Mexico City, and the young Andres without headband and huaraches was their conduit into that community. All episodes in Spanish.

Under "El es Dios INAH 1965" is also a link to "Pero ¡Ay Jesús!. Alabanza. Andrés Segura." The maestro is the lead singer and plays the *mandolina conchera* in this song of praise.

There is the classic two-hour lecture by the maestro at

DQU University in Sacramento in the late 1970's entitled "The Path of Quetzalcoatl." It is also titled "Tlamatini Andres Segura." This lecture features a long discussion on the life/death Duality, and there is a contemporaneous English translation to the maestro's Spanish presentation. This makes this video the best for English-only audiences. Two other known videos are "Calmecac Xochipilli: los cuatro vientos," and "El Maestro Andres Segura Granados Part 3." The second of these has the maestro lecturing in the English language.

4

What is the Red Road?

The "Red Road" is a modern term that refers to the worldviews/belief systems of the various and diverse Red Nations pueblos spread out from Alaska to Chile. Even though these thousands of Red Nations pueblos have their own version of the Red Road, there is enough commonality amongst them, that they can be deemed to constitute one Abya Yala native worldview. A belief system is also called a worldview or a religion. But the Red Road worldview is very different from the Middle East religions of Judaism, Christianity, and Islam. It does, however, share some similarities with both Buddhism and Hinduism.
What is a worldview and what is its purpose?

A worldview is how you see and relate to the world around you. A worldview is how you identify as an individual and with the culture you belong to. A worldview forms your beliefs as you grow older and react to life experiences. A worldview dictates how you interact with your family, your community, your country. A worldview provides a purpose for, and goals, to achieve a meaningful life. A worldview is how you visualize and perceive your relationship to the Absolute Being, or not. A worldview is what gives/doesn't give you belief in an afterlife. A worldview is like the rudder on a ship that enables you to get to the destination you seek.

Most religions have characteristics like dedicated ceremonies (mass, communion, puja), religious leaders (Pope, Ayatollah, Dalai

Lama), religious orders (priests, rabbis, imams, nuns, monks, reverends), and buildings of worship (temples, mosques, churches). Many religions also have prophets (Jesus, Mohammed, Moses, the Buddha). Most religions have "holy books/texts" like the Bible, Koran, Torah, the Sutras, the Vedas.

The Red Road has NONE of the above. It has none, because they are not needed to energize the one-to-one interactive relationship you have and develop with the Great Spirit, as you travel on the Red Road. That is why the Red Road is more a worldview than a religion. The Red Road was formulated since ancient times by our original pueblo ancestors. The sky above you is the ceiling of the Red Road cathedral. The cathedral is the Mother Nature that surrounds you. The formulation of this worldview began when the original pueblos considered their role within the environment and came to view Nature as their Mother; a Mother who not only protected them, but clothed and fed them as well.

Besides providing for the physical needs of our ancestors, Mother Nature also taught them how to live their lives harmoniously with the animals, the fish, the birds, and all living beings. Mother Nature taught our ancestors how to live reciprocally with the environment and other life forms. Mother Nature taught lessons that made the cosmos, the night sky, understandable. From all these experiences, our ancestors formulated their own versions of the Red Road.

The Red Road is a cosmic worldview for it honors the Four Directions. The Four Directions are the symbol/energy of the Universe, the Great Spirit, the Absolute Being. Four is also the colors humans manifest: Red, Black, Yellow and White. By honoring the Four Directions, the Red Road is expressing its cosmic integration beyond the Earthly confines of our solar system.

All the original pueblos of the Turtle continent and her southern sister, known as Abya Yala, share the same basic Red Nations worldview. They understand that their human lifetime also has a cosmic purpose. This basic worldview amongst all the native pueblos from Alaska to Chile, honoring Mother Nature with the cosmic purpose of promoting harmony, is known as the Red Road.

This worldview begins with a consciousness that Mother Earth is a living being, and that humans are part of her family. Calling her Mother Earth is more than a statement demonstrating how climate-change conscious you are. Rather, it is a recognition that this Earth environment all beings/organisms live on, is alive as well. When consciousness considers that Mother Earth is a living being, with her own soul and spirit, then it will understand that she also has a cosmic role and purpose. In order for Mother Earth to fulfill her cosmic role and purpose, she must place her own health above the interests of the organisms (i.e. humans) that live upon her. To humans, we call her health adjustments, "climate change."

Thus, Mother Earth is not subject to the will of humans, as the Europeans believe; but rather, humans are subject to the will of Mother Earth. Being part of her family means that humans are related to other organisms that live on Mother Earth. We depend on her environment and atmosphere in order to live. This is what is called a reciprocal relationship; humans and all the kingdoms give and take from each other to create one Existence. This understanding generates a consciousness that humans are not superior to any other life form. Instead, humans and other organisms are cooperators in the cosmic harmony that Mother Nature naturally provides.

The above are part of the philosophical foundations for the Red Road. A worldview formulated by generations of truth-seekers over centuries of observation and interaction. A scientific worldview formulated by being in intimate contact with a Mother Nature that was seen and treated as a mother, provider, and teacher. Because of their heightened awareness, our native ancestors were able to access an extraordinary knowledge from her, while marveling and questioning the constant diversity they were observing.

That is the goal for those Chicanos wishing to travel on the Red Road: to integrate knowledge from our ancestors and contemporary relatives to create their own version of this Road. As free human beings, as members of the pueblo of Aztlan within the Red Nations, as eternal spirits, Chicanos are thus empowered to create their own Chicano Red Road, to search for the meanings to their eternal lives.

Part Two

The
RED ROADS

Shoshone/Bannocks

The white people have come into my country, and have not asked my consent. Why is this?

...Chief Taghee

Preface to Shoshone/Bannock Ideology

This section comes from the writings of Dr. LaNada Warjack, a Shoshone/Bannock friend since our days as young students at UC Berkeley. Specifically, this section comes from her recent book, *"Native Resistance: An Intergenerational Fight for Survival and Life,"* (2019). In 1969, we were co-chairs of the Third World Liberation Front (TWLF) at Berkeley; she heading the Native American contingent and I the Chicano. From participation in that two-month strike, which together with the contemporaneous SF State TWLF strike, resulted in the establishment of Ethnic Studies nationwide, LaNada's activism continued with the Native American occupation of Alcatraz from 1969-71.

She has had a life-long involvement with Shoshone/Bannock issues against the US government at the Fort Hall reservation in Idaho where she lives. Not surprisingly, she comes from a family background of defiant Shoshone/Bannocks going back to the 1800's, including her great-grandfather, Tahmonmah (War Jack), the war chief during the Sheepeater campaign. She does not consider herself an academic, though she holds a PhD in political science. Because of her life-long involvement in Native American issues, she has spoken and participated at multiple gatherings on these topics throughout the country.

She defines the Great Spirit as the Universal Consciousness, a concept learned from her elders and prophesies. She learned and developed her worldview being exposed to a Mother Nature etiquette since childhood; spiritual individuals she has come contact with in; and participation in the Sun Dance. Her recitation of an indigenous ideology is important because of her background and because it comes from a current Native American woman. This is an organic natural worldview of a Red Nations person who has been raised and educated in this worldview within a Native environment in our modern times, and outside the influence of Christianity. Her Red Road is one of practice and use, not of theory.

Dr. Warjack's visualization of her indigenous ideology is less wordy than the more theoretical and philosophical presentations of the Mayan and Mexica Red Roads that follow. Yet, it still contains all of the most important components of any Red Road. She expresses this worldview naturally, as a person would, who has been raised with a firm belief in the native worldview and purpose of her pueblo; a community with roots thousands of years old in the Turtle continent, long before the European believed the world might possibly be round.

There is an undeniable unity between her worldview and the maestro's Mexica worldview, revealed in the movement of energy; *"our voices carry on the first rays of sunlight, which impacts the atoms to turn positive."* As to unity with the Mayan worldview, when she states that *"the Indigenous way of life developed from our science of nature;"* this is totally the approach the Mayans used to develop their science from the examples of Nature, which turned into their philosophy and religion. This should not be surprising, and again confirms that there was but one worldview amongst the Red Nations: that of balance, harmony, and reciprocity amongst all the forms of life of Mother Nature. Or, as Martinez Paredez states; "as cooperators in the cosmic harmony."

Her interpretation of indigenous ideology is set forth below in two components. The first is drawn from her book and the second, titled *"What is the Indigenous Ideology,"* is an outline she prepared to explain this worldview when she gives public presentations. You will notice that Dr. Warjack includes all indigenous peoples of the world who honor

Mother Nature, as being under her umbrella of an "indigenous ideology." The reader, thus, will have the opportunity to examine both outlines that comprise her Shoshonean/Bannock Red Road.

This first part, republished with her permission, is taken from *"Native Resistance: An Intergenerational Fight for Survival and Life,"* (pp. 19-21, 2019).

1

Shoshone/Bannock Red Road

"Since the inception of the European arrival, Native people have tried to promote and communicate an understanding of our natural laws that are connected to all life on Earth, taking only what is needed with prayers and respect. This Native worldview is universally consistent among all Indigenous people who maintain a positive understanding of, observe, and practice the natural laws of the planet.

Native people followed the seasons for their food. We ate the plants and animals that were geographic to our territories where we lived, and which became our medicines and symbols. Our people studied all forms of life in our environment, which connected us to the living ecosystem that surrounded us. The Indigenous way of life developed from our science of nature, which provided us with an understanding of how to best live together. Our purpose was not to accumulate personal wealth like Western society but to practice sharing and giving. If we had plenty, we had ceremonies and potlatches with which to be generous and share with our people.

We practiced the universal natural laws of how the plants and animals contributed and lived together. In this way, our judgment of how to govern ourselves was not prejudiced by greed or some immoral, unethical set of unjust principals. More than that, we recognized animals, birds, stones, trees, water, etc., that are alive with the same spirit that flows through both us and all life.

The recognition of all life-forms amplified the active principles in a world of personal relationships in which we related to them as our relatives and held a deep reverence of joy and love. We communicated and supported life through our prayers, songs, and dances. In turn, the plants and animals provided us with our food, homes, and positive way of life. Our entire ideology derived from this knowledge, which has preserved the continuous survival of our people and the land for tens of thousands of years.

This knowledge was universally known and practiced at one time as a common understanding among all indigenous people. We did not go into another village and see them as different, because a cultured people can recognize another cultured people— they just live in a different environment wherein different plants and animals are geographic to that environment, but used in the same way as medicines, clans, and symbols.

As individuals and societies, indigenous ideology is a natural and respectful interrelationship and connection with all life on Earth. Drummers and singers maintain a prayerful and concentrated positive thought through voice that gives strength in unison with the heartbeat of Mother Earth. This—combined with song—creates sound that comes from the heart and soul, flowing through the air on light.

As humans, we are the only species on earth that can combine voice with positive concentrated thought, creating sound combined with light to strengthen and activate people, plants, and animals in our sphere of space and dimension. The dances are movements of nature and animals combined with song and the heartbeat of Mother Earth to promote strength and positive growth for all life and abundance of food for harvest.

We emanate and imitate these sounds through dances and songs to support positive growth and balance. We consider animals as our relatives because we can see that our relationships with one another are evident, which makes us all stronger. The plants, animals, and all of nature are dependent on our actions to maintain a balance of life's energies. They receive the positive atoms in the air that flow from the heart and soul through human voice in prayer, songs, dances, and ceremonies.

The plants, animals, and all life that receive these powerful, encoded messages sent through the air depend on us for this continuous, supportive connection. We depend on the plants and animals for our food and survival, which is a personal, reciprocal relationship that extends to all people. This is how we conducted our daily lives on all levels to match the ebb and flow of life and the constant give and take of our relationships.

Working together with male and female energies and respecting the delicate balance of relationships through thought, action, word, and deed is nature's code of ethics. Our practice to maintain the balance of land and life is our goal as humans, and it is our responsibility to promote this continuous and positive interaction between all.

This knowledge is the matriarchy, which is how our original Indigenous tribal governments operated—by natural law. It is not man-made or written law because it is the balance of male and female energies and not male over female or female over male, but rather the balance of both that makes up the laws of the universe and how the living ecosystem interconnects and works with each other, which extends to all people. This is how we maintained peace between both ourselves and other tribal nations at one time."

2

What is Indigenous Ideology?

"The picture below shows a medicine symbol prevalent in most tribes who have been able to retain some knowledge and traditions practiced by their ancient culture. After the genocide and government stealing of all the children, they were placed into government and Christian boarding schools where they were brainwashed and assimilated by being denied their Native languages, culture, ceremonies and traditions. The physical, mental and sexual abuse suffered by these children left a scar of dysfunction coupled with extreme poverty on Indian reservations and urban strongholds.

What is still known by some tribes are that this sacred circle stands for the four races of humankind. All other nationalities are the combination of two or more of these races. Four is the sacred number of the directions, east, west, north and south. The four stages of life: infant; youth, adulthood and elderly. It is the four elements: fire; water; earth and air. Four also represents the seasons in the year: Spring; summer; fall and winter. It is the four medicines, tobacco, cedar, sweet grass and sage. Four has many meanings and is a medicine wheel. What the circle stands for is the sacred circle of life and we are all represented. What this means is that at one time, we were all in the sacred circle together sharing the same knowledge and spirituality.

The North and South American continents were the last to practice the natural laws of the Universe throughout thousands of years. The greatest civilizations on earth were the Inca, Maya and the Aztec. According to the Hopi prophesy, once the sacred laws were broken, it would mean the coming of the continents and great harm and destruction would fall upon the people. The Aztec priests upgraded their sacrifice to humans in an effort to avert the destruction of the earth. Other Aztec priests knew they had a limited time to implant the sacred roots of the nation throughout the lands in order to survive into the future.

Movements and migrations started north and south, then in all directions to accomplish this end. Those who stayed were obliterated when the Spanish arrived. Those who left their homes and cities migrated into uninhabited places throughout the continents and their generations are still alive today. These people are the Native tribes of North and South America. They are still trying to survive from the top of the earth, Alaska, Canada, America, Mexico down to the tip of South America, Brazil and the Amazon Rain Forests. These are all our Indigenous Native peoples.

The way we lived throughout our geographical ecosystem was by the environment, plants and animals that were there and by the natural laws of the living ecosystem in our physical location. We never considered our culture as different from one another because we could see that the environment allowed creation of practices, ceremonies, medicines, symbols and clans that appear different. However, a cultured person could always see another culture for the same survival and spiritual purposes. This is how we all lived with the natural laws at one time.

The way we learned the natural laws is by observing nature and how everything works together. When the trees start to turn red, we come down from the mountains because that tells us the snow is coming and it will be very cold soon. We move to the lower elevations where it is warmer to camp throughout the winter. In the spring we traveled the migratory routes to find game, berries and roots. We knew what time of the year our food would be ready to gather, hunt and fish. We respected other bands and tribal territories where we lived and often, we would harvest together.

We got together for harvest, ceremonies and trade. It was forbidden for clans to intermarry into the same clan lines so we always looked for other tribes as marital partners to strengthen our bloodlines. The names of our clans throughout the Uto-Aztecan Nation were for our plant or animal life that we ate and identified for our medicine and symbol. It was very important to respect all life because our very survival was dependent upon this.

An integral component to following the natural laws was preserving it for our future. We did this through songs, dances and prayers or ceremonies. As the only component, as humans in the living ecosystem, we are responsible to maintain life and keep the balance. This is done through sound, which comes from our heart and soul, through our mouths in the form of voice to create words and song. When we pray or sing, we maintain positive concentrated thought coupled with sound that carries on light to the plants, animals and other people who are waiting for these positive atoms to help them grow in a positive way and this is how we maintain balance.

When we dance, we dance together with the heartbeat of Mother Earth, which is emulated with the drumbeat to let the underworld know that we are maintaining our spiritual laws. We are singing and thinking of beautiful images to carry on sound, which support life. Where we conduct these ceremonies gives everything in the nearby area a good blessing for life.

Prayers to the Sun at dawn are for worldwide blessings. When we pray, dance and sing at sunrise, our voices carry on the first rays of sunlight, which impacts the atoms to turn positive. As the Sun goes around the Earth, the light carries these blessings to all life. We brought this ceremony from our ancient past, which we still practice today.

Indigenous Ideology was practiced worldwide at one time by all cultures. Throughout time, many of these practices have changed. As indigenous people, we all know that the Earth is our mother. The white tiger in China is sacred like the white buffalo in the Plains. We are all connected to the Earth through our ancient practices that have survived throughout the seven continents.

The new western civilization that has developed over the past five hundred years do not use natural laws but are made up to support the males and the very wealthy. It is a hierarchy of oppression that practices a made-up religion called Christianity and is not tied to the Earth. Western ideology is a way of thinking that does not respect life and is based on greed. Indigenous thought understands and knows respect for the Earth and all life."

The Yucatec Mayan Red Road

The theme cosmovision is very significant in the life of the Maya today, because our cosmovision opens a way to understand those around us. It teaches us how to be with all created beings that inhabit the cosmos.

>...Batz Lem
>K'akchiquel

Preface to Yucatec Mayan Red Road

Early in my relationship with the maestro Andres Segura Granados, he recommended that I read the books of Domingo Martinez Paredez. Upon doing so, I discovered that Paredez was swimming upriver in the academic world of Mexico, because of his views. Swimming upriver meant his views on the *indigena*, and the Maya more specifically, were the opposite of the accepted Western academic versions. He was competing academically, with little success, against the so-called Mexican giants like Garibay, Caso, and Leon-Portilla; who continued to parrot European versions. As opposed to these academicians, his were the organic views of a native, since Martinez Paredez was an Indian. A Mayan Indian who spoke several Mayan languages in addition to Nahuatl.

He came from an ancestral clan of Yucatec Mayan day-keepers and learned scholars called the H'menes, descendants of the even more ancient X'Tolob scholars. His mother was a Mayan *curandera* (shaman) from H'men lineage; and she practiced healing as well as spiritual *curanderismo*. A spiritual curandero works with the spirit world to accomplish goals. His father was technically a mestizo, which is why Paredez is also listed as mestizo. But his version of mestizo was to look as Indian as any Indian. This was a big problem within Mexican academia, which has historically denigrated the original pueblos of Mexico.

He became a philologist, which is the study of languages. His specialty was his native Yucatec Mayan, though he was proficient in the K'iche and K'akchikel Mayan languages of Guatemala. He was also fluent in Nahautl. He informed that the oral language of the Mayans, is very different from the written Mayan dictionaries invented by the Europeans. His skills at both interpreting the written metaphors in Mayan literature, and navigating the errors caused by erroneous dictionaries; revealed the true intentions of the Mayan writers. Overcoming numerous academic hurdles both because of his views as well as his looks, he became Professor of Mayan Studies at the UNAM, Mexico's national university. He was also the Mayan maestro of my maestro.

The maestro Andres made it a point to stress that the Mayan pueblo was the Grandmother/Grandfather culture of the Red Nations. By this he meant that the ancient Mayan nation was literally the philosophical roots of the Red Nations; the discoverers of the science of Mother Nature that today has become known as the Red Road. When I undertook to collect and then translate five of the Paredez books, **"The Domingo Martinez Paredez Mayan Reader,"** (2017); I finally had the opportunity to understand the depth of knowledge that Martinez Paredez shared in his writings.

When the maestro introduced me to the Mexica worldview of *La Esencia de las Cosas*, my immediate reaction was that the worldview he was painting was very scientific in its explanation and application. This was frankly a shock because I had never considered that the native nature-based worldview would have anything to do with science. My initial reaction/intuition regarding the scientific nature of this native worldview he was describing turned out to be correct. It turned out to be correct because the Mayan worldview the Mexica eventually incorporated was totally scientific and evolutionary in its development; and was, I would discover, the genesis of the maestro's "*la Esencia de las Cosas.*"

Here is Martinez Paredez confirming the role of the spirit and the Serpent, and why the Mayan philosopher viewed and honored the spirits of nature, rather than considering them "gods" as the Spanish claimed;

(***"The Popol Vuh Has Reason"***, p.278):

"His wise men proceed to acquire great and marvelous knowledge. When he founded his religion, he did not invent and create deities urged by his simple imagination, but instead these were born by that reason that every element of nature is a cooperator to cosmic harmony. Thus arises the Lord of Energy, Can or Chan, the serpentine symbol of excellence. This Chan becomes the fundamental basis on which rests Philosophy, Religion and Science, linked together intimately, since each facet is part of the greater Whole, which is represented through the figure of the reptile, representative of Creative Energy."

Martinez Paredez confirmed many aspects of the maestro's Mexica worldview; albeit spread out over several books and presented in academic form. He painted a picture of how the Mayan worldview was developed; a worldview which in pursuit of the Truth used and found within the Science of Nature their answers. This Science in turn became their truths/Philosophy; and both morphed together to create their beliefs, their Religion.

This worldview was developed over centuries while maintaining a constant evolutionary vision of the Earth and reaching an understanding of a Universe with a measurable Existence. A worldview with the ability to measure Existence, because of the mathematics the Mayan scholars developed, to place themselves within eternity. A worldview able to understand a Universe founded on complementary Dualities, which has proceeded to express Itself in Diverse never-ending forms into apparent eternity.

Because of his views, Paredez was not very well known, even in Mexico, when he died in 1984. Three years later, in 1987, Jose Arguelles published "The Mayan Factor," which became an international New Age best seller. Because Arguelles made reference to some ideas of Martinez Paredez in his book, Martinez Paredez became tainted by the New Age community's promoters and opponents three years AFTER his death. This New Age *mentirero* (pack of lies) is tantamount to a Mormon post-mortem baptismal. In other words, dismiss the New Age chatter of Martinez-Paredez, as *chisme* (gossip) of the first degree.

I highly recommend that *indigenistas* read Martinez Paredez. You will discover nuggets of native history including the links between the pueblos of Mexico and South America. You will learn how the Mayans used allegory to write the **"Popol Vuh;"** and what they really meant by the stories contained therein. He will surprise you by explaining why the written Mayan dictionaries are really a European-invented language full of errors, and very different from the everyday oral language of the Mayans. You will dive into the comparisons of Mayan philosophy to other belief systems in the world. He will reveal little known histories of the Toltecs, Mexicas, and the beginnings of the Mexican identity and nation.

The Yucatec Mayan Red Road that I present below is mostly taken from excerpts from several of his books. I added some chile with the Chan. The more I read and understood his material, the clearer it became that Martinez Paredez was painting a picture of a worldview made possible by a disciplined and inquisitive body of learned ancient Mayan scholars. A worldview that methodically incorporated the Science Mother Nature revealed, which in turn expressed itself as a Philosophy seeking more knowledge, and which Truths gradually became accepted as their Religion. All three were intimately interwoven by the Serpent, the exoteric representative of Creative Energy within the Great Spirit, manifesting itself as their Science, Philosophy, and Religion.

Having been exposed to the Mexica worldview in 1972 and recognizing its focus on the movement and transformation of energy, I found the Mayan worldview to be egalitarian in comparison. The Mayans were essentially dreamers and idealists, always searching to find the harmonious balance amongst all forms of life. The Mayans took to heart their findings that the human is not superior to any other organism in Nature, but instead is equal to all other organisms, all harmoniously living together as "cooperators of the cosmic harmony." In comparison, the Mexica were definitely more focused and structured, and not dreamers in the expression of their worldview.

The Mayan civilization is thousands of years old; how many thousands is in debate. The Mayan pueblo is associated with the domestication of corn, and that happened over 9,000 years ago. There was arguably an even earlier civilization, the **Tamoanchoas**, who were a proto-Mayan pueblo who conceptualized the Feathered Serpent, and predated the Olmecs, those of the large stone heads, and the *Teotihuacanos* who built Teotihuacan. The Toltecs would come later, as well as others like the Mexica.

Given the age of this pueblo, it is reasonable to conclude that there were periods of significant advances, and periods where the society languished and forgot prior achievements. The Mayans achieved much of their knowledge thousands of years ago, when no other Red Nations pueblo was articulating the science of nature the Mayans were able to discover. The present-day repository of native knowledge in the United States, the Hopi, have within their oral tradition that several Mayan clans left the Yucatan and joined them in approximately year 1000.

The Mayans reached the zenith of their creative civilization in the year 900. This was six hundred years BEFORE the Spaniard appeared. Thus, those Mayans collaborating with the Spaniards in the 1500's were reciting a long-forgotten history. Mayan history shows that they were not "empire-builders," and essentially warred amongst themselves rather than against other pueblos.

While the Mayans were not empire-builders, they were cosmic travelers. They employed skills unknown to the Western world in their pursuit of the truth. Their disciplined scholars, the X'Tolob, were always seeking to understand the complex integration of the human being with the cosmic sky. **How could they not have come to the conclusion that the human is part of the same night sky that she/he sees every night?**

Note: there exists a speculative relationship between the Mayans and the ancient Hindus of India. The maestro Andres alluded on more than one occasion that in ancient times, some Mayan masters had connected with Hindu masters in the dream and spirit world, resulting in the significance and use of the name/phrase "Maya," in various Hindu philosophical beliefs and texts.

1

PANCHE BE:
the Search for the Roots of the Truth

      This story begins in the ancient Mayan lands of the Yucatan and Guatemala, soon after corn had been domesticated around 9,000 years ago. With a now certain supply of food, the ancient Mayan communities had the luxury to allow persons to express their individuality within the pueblos. Within the diversity of the pueblos, learned teachers, called the X'Tolob, began to appear. A call went out to have the X'Tolob gather periodically from all the Mayan pueblos, so that they could ponder the mysteries of Life and the Universe on behalf of their people. After many years of gathering and deliberation, the X'Tolob arrived at a methodology to secure the answers they sought.

      The methodology they employed in their search for the answers to their questions was called Panche Be (Paan-che Be{tter}). In the Yucatec Mayan language, Panche Be means to "search for the roots of the truth." Philosophically, to make such a statement evidences the depth of thinking involved, and its connection to Mother Nature. This methodology postured that for every possible truth people believed in, there were reasons for and against, that potential truth. Using Panche Be, all the possible reasons/roots for any truth were methodically considered, analyzed, and debated; before deciding if that root/reason justified/did not justify the proposed Truth. This was the methodology employed by the X'Tolob in their Panche Be investigations.

To understand this concept, let's consider a tree as a possible truth. You can see the tree trunk and branches above the ground (believed truth), but you can't see below the ground to ascertain the roots of the tree (the reasons for and against the belief). Before the X'Tolob accepted that tree with what their eyes told them, they mentally dug underneath Mother Earth to expose the roots of that tree. This was the Panche Be exercise; to search for the reasons (roots) for that truth (tree), before deciding if it was a truth or not. In other words, they didn't jump to conclusions as to any believed truth. Instead, they thoroughly considered all possibilities, before deciding whether it was a truth or not.

As part of their Panche Be investigations to discover their truths, the X'Tolob used many tools now long forgotten. One tool was the ability to communicate with the animal and the natural world. All organisms have souls and spirits; and this meant that other forms of interaction were possible than the use of human language. Another tool was the ability to manipulate energy. Manipulating energy meant they had the ability to create a nahual body and shift their consciousness into that nahual body. They could thus create animal images of themselves and assume all the medicine/energy and capabilities that animal/bird possessed. Manipulating energy also meant they could secure cooperation from various relatives in nature for their search for the roots of the truth.

They also used the dream world to travel throughout the Universe. In their dreams, their disciplined consciousnesses could travel wherever it desired since consciousness is spirit, and thus free to move as energy. Having a disciplined consciousness meant they were conscious of dreaming when dreaming, which meant they could instantly launch that consciousness wherever they desired. They could also perform feats while dreaming that would have been impossible with a physical body.

The dream world thus offered the X'Tolob the opportunity to interact with the Universe, to search for, or confirm, their findings. The X'Tolob also used the dream world to communicate with the spirit world, on a regular basis in their search for the roots of any truth. The point here is that the X'Tolob went way beyond relying on the everyday Western vision of life, which limits itself to the senses of feeling, tasting, smelling, touching, and seeing.

While these tools may seem fantastical to the Western mind, it is only because Western culture chooses to see Reality very narrowly, like a horse with blinders. In the native mind of the X'Tolob, the world they were interacting with on a daily basis, was a world of energy in evolution, with its own will. The X'Tolob were literally Living their lives as a part of Nature, daily interacting with Nature on a reciprocal basis, as all the animal/other kingdoms did, rather than being a detached observer to the unfolding of Life before them.

The initial calculation of the X'Tolob, was to determine *"what is a Truth?"* After deliberations, they came to the conclusion that a Truth is a belief accepted by the large majority of people. Some truths were obvious and did not require much search for the reasons for their existence. Some of these obvious early truths were that the dawn brings light, and dusk starts the night. Our bodies need sleep. Water evaporates. Rain wets. Fire burns. Staring at the Sun will blind you. These and other similar examples were the easy truths accepted by all the pueblos.

In their Panche Be searches, the X'Tolob did not speculate as the European philosophers did. Instead, they exercised a rigorous examination, a scientific approach, of the evidence before them. This evidence was gathered from both the physical and the spirit world, before they arrived at a decision regarding any truthfulness. Mother Nature was the Teacher that provided the evidence, the science, of the material world. The spirit world provided the explanations that confirmed the physical findings of the material world.

For the physical evidence of the material world, the X'Tolob observed and interacted with Mother Nature for centuries, before acknowledging the existence of a consistent cycle of Life. The cycle of Life they observed, was that most Life on Earth comes from a seed or an egg. The seed/egg then evolves, entering stages of Life that can be defined as infancy, youth, maturity, aging, and death.

However, the Mayan death was not the European death, meaning the end of life. Instead, the Mayan death was a transformation of the consciousness leaving the material human body and returning to spirit as energy. Continuing its transformation in the spirit world, the spirit would transform back into human form in a future lifetime. In other words, the Mayan death was the complementary half of eternal cycles of life/death. For the Mayans, Death is needed to bring new Life; without it, Life cannot exist.

The X'Tolob came to this conclusion because they saw that the "death" of an aged plant was really a *transformation* of the plant. The plant didn't just disappear. Instead, the "dying plant" had already shed its seeds to generate future life before disintegrating into the fertilizer for a new plant. This dual transformation of the aged plant was a cycle that brought new life that would itself age and bring new life again.

The X'Tolob thus reasoned that the old plant was energy, energy that was transforming into new energy manifested by the young plant. This new energy would eventually age and die/transform into another new energy. This cycle of the transformation of energy, they confirmed over many years, repeated itself faithfully throughout Mother Nature.

The spirit world provided confirmation that the life/death cycle the X'Tolob were observing, was a consistent feature of Life. This cycle of energy eternally transforming itself, is the process of evolution. Evolution also incorporates the new energies each previous cycle has produced. This was the Truth of Evolution that the X'Tolob arrived at. This was confirmed through a Panche Be investigation into the roots of that believed truth. As part of that Panche Be investigation into evolution, the X'Tolob determined that Life began on Earth when the four elements of Fire, Water, Air, and Earth, united.

The X'Tolob used the Hurricane to express these findings in visualizing the birth of Life on Earth. In their rendition of the birth of Life, a mist above the oceans covered everything; nothing else was visible; everything was still. Below this quiet mist, the Earth slowly rose from amongst the waters when the temperature of the Earth had cooled. Over time, Air appears, as Earth's soul has created an atmosphere which envelopes her.

With its swirling winds, Air gathers both Water and Earth particles within the funnel of the Hurricane. These Water and Earth particles were then energized by the bolts of lightning (Fire), that thundered within the power of the Hurricane. The now Fired (energized) Water and Earth particles were then blown far and wide by the Hurricane's winds. The X'Tolob concluded that these particles were the original energized seeds of Life that arose from the Unity of the four elements.

The four elements of Air, Water, Fire and Earth are also called the classical elements, because they appear throughout the world in different cultures as part of creation myths. Indeed, the human body is composed mostly of Water, will turn to dust (Earth) upon decomposing, and to live, maintains a body temperature (Fire), and breaths Air to nourish the blood and organs. Thus, the X'Tolob concluded that humans and all life on Earth were the result of evolution, since all organisms come from her soil and waters, and are energized by the two other elements of Fire and Air.

Once the X'Tolob felt comfortable that the cycle of Life they were constantly experiencing/observing was a regular part of Mother Nature, and that Life began on Earth due to evolution, they turned their eyes towards the sky. *"Were the examples of Life they were observing on Mother Earth applicable to the Universe?"*

Seeking an answer, the most challenging early questions the X'Tolob faced came from the night sky. *"Is there such a thing as a Universe? How did the Universe begin? Who created the Universe? What sustains the Universe?"* These were all questions that required the X'Tolob to determine the origins of the Universe, in order to better understand the evolution they had found.

To test their beliefs, the X'Tolob extrapolated Mother Nature's lessons in their search to understand the origins of the Universe. To extrapolate means to make a mathematical estimate of how something small, will be, if it was bigger. In this case, the X'Tolob extrapolated their findings on Earth as to the seed/egg beginnings and applied them to the Universe.

Extrapolating the concept of a seed to consider the birth of the Universe, the X'Tolob created the mathematical symbol of Zero, which represented the Seed of the Universe. This symbolism was based once again on the logic/examples of Mother Earth. "If life begins with a seed/egg on Earth, then Life in the Universe should also have begun with a seed/egg," the X'Tolob calculated.

The Zero was purposely drawn as a seed on their glyphs, so that people would understand that the Universe had also spawned from a seed. Being a seed symbolized that the Zero, the Universe-to-be, was in dormant or latent form. Being latent means that all the energy of Life within the Seed was there, but it was asleep. Thus, the Mayan Zero represented the unconscious Everything; or the Idea waiting to happen.

Projecting that the Universe was created from the latent Seed of Existence, the X'Tolob next pondered how that latent Seed became active. **"How and why did that Universal Seed suddenly wake up?"** The spirit world provided the answer to this question. The spirit world communicated that the activation of the Universal Seed came from the unconscious Cosmic Consciousness spontaneously becoming conscious of Itself.

With this knowledge, the X'Tolob visualized the birth of the Universe. It began when the Cosmic Consciousness of the Great Spirit spontaneously awoke from its latent stage, became conscious of Itself, and then used Its now evolved Consciousness to create a Vision of Creation. The continuing evolution of a now fully conscious Cosmic Consciousness, then activated the Vision of Creation, to give birth to the Universe.

Satisfied that they had a credible understanding of the birth of the Universe, the X'Tolob in their usual scientific manner, set about to confirm these beliefs. The scientific manner they used to confirm these beliefs, was to create their own mathematics. Mayan mathematics are based on the vigesimal system, meaning the number 20 is the foundational number of their calculations. Other mathematical systems in the world are based on the number 10 as the foundational number.

Manipulating numbers 0-19 and the foundational 20, enabled the Mayans to create the most precise calendars known to mankind, especially in regards astronomy. Their mathematics also allowed the Maya to mathematically categorize/structure Life on Earth, by assigning values to all material forms and occurrences.

With this knowledge, the X'Tolob once again extrapolated their findings on Earth to the Universe, in order to understand the structure and flow of the Universe. They started by establishing the Zero as the starting point of the Universe, which allowed them to mathematically calculate Time from the beginning of Existence. Calculating Existence meant that the X'Tolob were able to measure time since the Universe began, which in turn proved the existence of the Great Spirit. The Mayans remain unique amongst the populations on Earth as the only community to KNOW that the Great Spirit exists; a knowledge gained from their mathematics. Every other culture on Earth, has used speculation and intuition, to formulate the existence of the Absolute Being.

Being able to calculate Existence, meant that the X'Tolob could now create various calendars, to understand and measure the cycles of the Universe. By this time, the X'Tolob had confirmed that cyclicity is the form of movement the Universe manifests. They developed several calendars in order to pursue their Panche Be investigations into the cyclical cosmos. One of these calendars, the Tzolkin, measured the integration of the newly born human being into the cosmos. The two most important numbers used for this Tzolkin integration calendar were 20 and 13. **Why?**

The human body has 10 fingers, and 10 toes, or 20 digits. The human body also has 13 joints. Each arm and leg have three joints, for a total of 12 joints. The neck is the 13th joint. Thus, the X'Tolob concluded, since it is these features of the human body which allow it to move and interact in so many ways, with the environment of Mother Nature; what could be more logical than using the corresponding numbers, to measure how this new-born baby will be integrated into the Universe? In this manner, the circumstances/date, and the night sky of the birth, were considered in using the Tzolkin. But this calendar is so precise, that even the circumstances present between the parents nine months earlier, when conception occurs, is considered when assessing the destiny of the newborn.

Continuing with a new Panche Be investigation, the X'Tolob now sought to confirm further information from the spirit world, regarding the Universal structure of Duality, by once again considering the examples of Mother Nature. Everywhere they looked in Mother Nature, they found complementary Dualities. There was always two ways of looking/considering the same thing. Not only were these two different ways always present, but each also depended on the existence of the other, for it to exist. That is what made them complementary Dualities. Being complementary demanded that there be a balance and harmony between the two.

As part of their investigation into Duality, the X'Tolob expressed the Mayan Great Spirit, as the Duality of the "One and the Many." This was both a mathematical and philosophical visualization of the Universe, with the "One" representing the sole Great Spirit, and the "Many," the Diversity of the Great Spirit. The "One and the Many" are complementary to each other, since the Great Spirit is both diverse and the sole Great Spirit, at the same time. The X'Tolob came to understand the Diversity of the Great Spirit by visualizing all of Existence as being composed of numbers, which were then assigned to represent a part of Existence. Their mathematical conclusion from this exercise, was that the "One and the Many," are two Parts of one Whole.

Note: this is a good opportunity to examine the different definitions of an "individual" from a native vs. European perspective. For a native, being an individual necessarily includes being part of a group, and thus, the individual within an original pueblo perspective identifies as "me/we." In contrast, the European promotes the individual over the community, and thus, the individual identifies with "me/my ego." These two very different definitions of what an individual is, has continued to manifest itself into the historical tension between the gabacho and the Mexican.

Since they concluded that mathematically the "One and the Many" are two Parts of One Whole, philosophically this confirmed that the "One and the Many" are complementary. Within this Duality, the "One" was Hunab K'u, while Hunac K'u represented the "Many." This "One and the Many" worldview later lay the foundation for **"In Lak'Ech"** (You are my Other Me). **"In Lak'Ech"** was an evolution of the philosophical conclusion that the Great Spirit is the "One and the Many," meaning the Great Spirit manifests multiple dualities within Diversity. The Mayans understood that the individual can only harmoniously be an individual, when that individual is part of a group. In return, the group is nourished and energized by the individuals that form the group.

Contrast this balanced worldview with the Western worldview which promotes the "One" over the "Many." In the Western world, the "One" (ego) finds constant justification to be exalted over the "Many" (community). Western thought hasn't yet realized that the "One" can only be a conscious "One," because of the interaction the "Many" provides to the "One;" meaning they are complementary to each other. The Mayans thought and understood better: the "One and the Many" both need each other, in order for each to exist and thrive.

Because the X'Tolob used mathematics to confirm all their findings, they used the geometric figures of a Square within a Circle, to represent Hunab K'u, who otherwise has no image. In this geometric representation, Hunab K'u was known as the Sole Giver of Movement and Measurement. Here the Circle (which has no beginning, nor end) represents Movement, or eternal Life. The Square within the Circle of Eternity is the Measurement of that movement, or Life. Thus, the Sole Giver of Movement and Measurement is Hunab K'u, for only the Great Spirit can grant measured Lives.

This, thus, was the history and role of the X'Tolob. To search for answers to the many questions our ancient Mayan ancestors had. They performed their searches in a manner consistent with a thorough scientific analysis, not through mere speculation. Of course, they also had resources long forgotten or ignored/unknown by modern persons. The ability to visualize a world of energy, the ability to manipulate this energy, the ability to access the Universe through the dream world, the ability to communicate with the spirit world.

Their Panche Be investigations were carried out with a long-term approach, meaning information/findings were passed onto future generations of X'Tolob until the Truths were established. They conducted these investigations thousands of years ago, when no other Red Nations pueblo had yet advanced their civilizations in order to provide help with these searches. The Mayans were the pathfinders for the Red Nations, when it came to the science of nature and the repository of native knowledge. As their knowledge of the science of Mother Nature became clearer and deeper, it became apparent to the X'Tolob that there is a definite pattern and structure to the Universe that can be understood. For the X'Tolob, the best place to find the answers to this pattern and structure of the Universe was Mother Nature.

2

Mother Nature:
The Great Provider and Teacher

The first life-sustaining role Mother Nature played for the humans of the Red Nations was that of the great provider. Mother Nature provided the earliest homes of caves and grottos, before humans made other structures. These caves and grottos provided humans with protection from both the predatory beasts as well as the early raging storms and inclement weather. Mother Nature also provided the first clothing for humans, taken from animal skins and plants.

Beyond protection and clothing, Mother Nature provided humans with their foods, taken from the plants as well as the meat of animals and fish. Perhaps more importantly, Mother Nature provided the essential water and clean air that was necessary for all Life to exist. For the early native searching for reassurance amongst all the challenges of the environment they found themselves in, Mother Nature was the provider which took them into her womb and provided them with shelter, food, clothing and water. All of these made their life possible amongst the challenging environments of the early Earth.

The early native thus considered Mother Nature as being their protector and provider. This view of Mother Nature is in direct contrast to Christianity, which views Nature as the Evil who introduced Original Sin to Adam and Eve, and thus, mankind. That is the reason

Christianity and the European have treated the Earth as an enemy to be conquered and exploited at will. In contrast, for the native of the Red Nations, there was no reason to consider Mother Nature as an enemy or as a threat to humans in any form. To the contrary, she was considered logically as the Mother who gave life to all her species and sustained the diversity of life that lived upon her. The native considered all the species as her children, a belief confirmed by the X'Tolob when they discovered evolution as the cause of all Life.

But Mother Nature went beyond providing for her children; she educated them as well. Everyday life/the environment were her classrooms, you could say she homeschooled all her children. Her "golpes de la vida" (blows/lessons of life) were the methodology she used that enabled humans to learn from their experiences, and thus be able to live a more meaningful lifetime. She gave lessons on how to live a harmonious life by respecting the right to life of all other species. She gave lessons on the importance of harmony and balance amongst her environments. Take only what you need.

Within harmony and balance, Mother Nature offered lessons on the use of medicine. She taught humans which plant relatives were useful for any type of human ailment. She taught humans the different types of medicine our animal relations also have, a different kind of medicine than from plants but medicine, nevertheless. Some of the animal medicine was so powerful that to use it put the user at great risk. She taught humans to feel and hear the thump of her own heartbeat, in order to discover which spots upon her lands held special energy. These locations of special energy were where dances, prayers, and worship were most powerful.

She taught lessons that humans are not superior to any other child of Mother Earth. She gave lessons on how humans and all the other kingdoms are living a reciprocal existence. She gave lessons that humans are cosmic beings, flying in space alongside her. Lessons that all living forms/beings on Mother Earth are cooperators in the cosmic harmony. Life lessons that could be confirmed by the stars in order to understand the rhythm of Life. Lessons that revealed the existence of her soul and spirit.

The revelation of the Earth's soul and spirit was the result of the X'Tolob's investigation into whether Earth was a living being. Using the dream world to travel into space, enabled the X'Tolob to ascertain that Mother Earth has an aura surrounding her. The X'Tolob instantly recognized the aura as Mother Earth's soul. Following their knowledge of Duality, this confirmed that the Earth also has a spirit.

Note: the Western world, while now beginning to focus on climate-change, continues to fail to recognize that Earth is a living being. All the changes in climate, and pandemics like covid-19 and its variants, are being initiated by Mother Earth to protect her health from the destructive actions of humans. Mother Earth has her own cosmic duties to perform, and these require that she maintain a healthy environment, however drastic her actions to do so may seem to humans.

Once the X'Tolob concluded this investigation with a firm Truth, that Mother Earth is a living being, because she has both a soul and a spirit; the Mayan worldview of her as Mother, became Unbreakable. The Mayans loved the landscape of her dress, which was Mother Nature, as a precious gift. They planted their crops and danced their dances by feeling her heartbeat. They gathered their medicines from her plants and their animal relatives.

To celebrate the Diversity their Mother provided, the Mayans created dances, songs, poetry, ceremonies, and flowers for all the aspects of Mother Nature. The X'Tolob taught their pueblos that Mother Nature was a treasure to be cared for and kept jealously in the company of the Lords of each of her Elements. They knew that in the mention of the names of their spirits, existed the Magic of their Life experience. To forget them would be like committing suicide. They never forgot, thus, that their Lords were different spirits of Mother Nature, not gods.

The wind was honored. The bear. The jaguar. The mountains. The eagles. The lakes. The serpent. The birds. The trees and other plant relatives. The reptiles. The fish. The moon. The many faces of Father Sun. The many phases of Mother Earth. These and many more aspects of their Life were celebrated in a year-long cycle of ceremonies and celebrations. The X'Tolob educated the people that all these

Lords/aspects of Mother Nature being celebrated were spirits, and as such they were all part of the Great Spirit.

But the X'Tolob were not satisfied with just being observers and celebrants of Nature. They were observing life around them and knew in their gut, that there was a reason why everything seemed to be in harmony and have a flow to it. They could sense an order to Life, they could feel the thumping heartbeat of the Universe, they marveled at the cycles of the stars and the constellations. They began to question whether a human is living a cosmic lifetime beyond Mother Earth's environment. ***"Do we have a cosmic purpose,"*** they wondered?

Pursuing this question, the X'Tolob found the supreme representative of the cosmic purpose they sought. That representative was the Serpent. The Serpent was the exoteric representative of the Great Spirit as Creative Energy, since it encapsulated Duality in many forms. It lived both in the water as well as on land. The Serpent was constantly transforming, emulating the life/death cycle, by shedding its skin multiple times throughout the year. It's undulating form of movement on Earth was replicated in the night sky by the form and movement of the constellations and galaxies. For these reasons and others, the Serpent became the representative of the Creative Energy that illuminated mankind's path to the cosmos.

Seeking to integrate themselves into the cosmos, the X'Tolob used the Serpent symbolism to create the first Bird Serpent duality. This original Duality consisted of the Earth and the Sun, our parents in the cosmic sky. In this Duality, Mother Earth was the Serpent, and Father Sun the Bird. The Bird Serpent duality was a recognition of the relationship between the planet which creates our bodies, and the Sun which provides the consciousness/spirit to give us Life. Since these parents who give us Life fly in the cosmic sky, the X'Tolob reasoned, mankind also flies in the sky, and as such is a cosmic being.

This Bird Serpent duality was known amongst the Maya as K'uukulcan. Thousands of years later, this Bird/Serpent duality would be known amongst the Nahuas/Mexicas, as the Feathered Serpent, Quetzalcoatl.

3

The Cosmic Consciousness- to Believe, Create, & Do

Feeling secure in their relationship as part of Mother Nature's family, and empowered by the effectiveness of their Panche Be methodology, the X'Tolob began to ask new questions of themselves: ***"Where does Thought come from? What is the purpose of thought/ prayer? Are humans the only form of life that thinks?"*** For the X'Tolob, thought and prayer/song were the same thing, since they both involved the intentional movement of energy. Seeking answers to their questions, the X'Tolob launched a Panche Be investigation by making distinctions between basic intelligence and thought, which they categorized as Creative Thought.

They defined basic intelligence as that intelligence Mother Nature has given all her children through evolution in order for them to survive and lead a purposeful life. This basic intelligence is used by all the animal, bird, fish and insect kingdoms to function and survive within their environments. Part of this basic intelligence forms the reciprocal relationship humans have with the various kingdoms. Some basic intelligence can be very complex and impressive. Humans also have the same type of intelligence. This includes the basic intelligence of eating correctly, drinking water, getting sleep and rest, and maintaining a healthy body and mind.

But humans have another type of intelligence which the X'Tolob came to define as Creative Thought. Humans also seem to be the only species who have Creative Thought. This Creative Thought goes beyond even the most complex basic intelligence. With Creative Thought, humans have built multiple forms of transportation, large irrigation systems, and cities. Humans have built civilizations and waged complicated wars on each other. Humans have domesticated animals and grains for their needs and food sources. Humans drew their earliest thoughts on cave walls. Humans have long discussed the stars and the night sky. Humans have discovered and use mathematics. Humans have considered the existence of a Great Spirit. Humans ask questions like ***"why am I living a lifetime?"***

The X'Tolob concluded that these human actions were examples of Creative Thought. All life forms have basic intelligence to live their lives. But the Creative Thought of humans is special. The X'Tolob wanted to know how Creative Thought worked. They wanted to know if Creative Thought had a role to play within Mother Nature and the cosmos. They wanted to find the structure of Creative Thought so it could be replicated and used to move energy towards an intended purpose.

The X'Tolob thus launched a Panche Be investigation into the Truth of Creative Thought. The examples of human events and history had already confirmed that Creative Thought existed. But the Panche Be investigation demanded that they determine where Creative Thought came from. By determining its origins, the X'Tolob reasoned, they might be able to replicate Creative Thought at will. These were scholars used to moving energy in their mathematical world, and the energy of Creative Thought was very attractive. As they pondered its origins, it became apparent to them that the answer lay at the start of the Universe. Indeed, they concluded that it was, in fact, Creative Thought which created the Universe.

They determined that the genesis of Creative Thought is to be found within the Cosmic Consciousness. The X'Tolob visualized that Creative Thought within the Cosmic Consciousness was the latent force within the Seed of Existence waiting to happen. It was latent because

It was unconscious. The X'Tolob compared the latent force within the Seed to being an unconscious Idea. In this comparison, the unconscious Cosmic Consciousness was an Idea that needed to be activated, so that it could become an Idea. The activation of the Idea occurred when spontaneous consciousness came to the Cosmic Consciousness. Now activated, the Idea (Creative Thought) flowered, and expressed Itself as Creation.

The X'Tolob thus concluded that the Cosmic Consciousness is the source of all Creative Thought. Said another way, the Cosmic Consciousness is both the roots and the branches of the Creative Thought tree. All fruit that grows on this tree, which includes all the knowledge of scientific and medicinal truths, the knowledge of astrophysics and higher mathematics, the knowledge for engineering feats, the creativity for music, the arts, cuisine; all knowledge useful for the betterment of Existence, gets their sustenance from their Cosmic Consciousness roots.

The Cosmic Consciousness is thus the Consciousness of the Great Spirit. Owing to their investigations, the X'Tolob were able to discover the formula for activating Creative Thought from the Cosmic Consciousness, so that humans could replicate it. The formula involved moving energy in a three-step process in order to achieve a desired result. This formula followed the same methodology/steps the unconscious Cosmic Consciousness had used to become Conscious of Itself, and thus create the Universe. In the Yucatec Mayan language, this formula is called MEN.

MEN is a phrase/concept that encompasses the three-step process of Believe, Create, and Do. To Believe is the first step of MEN and means to Believe in an idea, a desired end. For any idea/desire to ever become a reality, you must first form a Belief in this idea; you must want to see it come to fruition. With this first step of to Believe, you are moving energy by your INTENT in seeing your idea/desire become a reality. But if all you do is give birth to this idea, just "dream" about it, and never take any steps to make this idea a reality, it will remain nothing more than an idea. An idea/desire that will age and eventually be forgotten and discarded.

For this Belief to grow beyond an idea, you must move energy again by taking a second step. This second step entails Creating the environment for your idea to grow. Whatever your idea/desire may be, it requires an environment (the right circumstances) in which it can grow. You Create this environment by the steps you take to make your idea a reality. To Create is like preparing the soil so your seed can grow.

Say you want to become a *curandero/a* (shaman healer). That is your Belief, your idea. If you do nothing else, this desire will remain only an idea. To take the second step of MEN, you must Create the potential for your idea to happen by securing a teacher of *curanderismo* and immersing yourself in understanding the world of native healing. But your Belief/desire will stay an idea, even after you Create the soil for it to grow, unless you take the critical third step of MEN, which is to Do.

To Do in this case is to Act as a healer. Once again, you must move the energy involved in being a healer by performing this third step as a healer. Only after completing all three steps of MEN, to Believe, Create, and Do; will your idea become a reality. The third step of MEN, to Do, is often the most difficult step of MEN. Ideas enter our minds almost daily (Believe), and our minds can begin to justify/visualize Creating the environment for our desire/idea to happen, but most ideas die without fully developing the Create stage. To actually act, Do, on any idea, is the greatest challenge for most persons.

The MEN formula was based on the three-step process the X'Tolob visualized happened at the beginning of the Universe. The idea, the Belief, of the Universe was contained within the Cosmic Consciousness, which then awoke and started to Create a vision of Existence. The final step was when the Cosmic Consciousness actually Did and turned the vision into Creation.

There remained two questions the X'Tolob had not answered. They were **"what is the purpose of Thought?"** and "are humans the only species which can think?" From a material perspective, it was obvious that Creative Thought had made possible all the advances the Mayan civilization had attained, including cures for diseases, their impressive cities, and scientific advancements. But the X'Tolob were asking these questions from a spiritual perspective, because the journey of the human spirit was always the primary consideration in their deliberations. They were really asking, *"what is the purpose of thought in our spiritual journey?"*

They found the answer to both questions when they considered thoughts/prayers/songs/dances from the perspective of cosmic harmony. If you consider Creative Thought as the ability to access the Cosmic Consciousness, the human is the only species which can access the Cosmic Consciousness, the X'Tolob concluded. They further reasoned that the human has this ability, because it is the role of humans as a cooperator in the cosmic harmony, to activate the atoms in the air with positive energy, for the benefit of all the species. The activation of positive energy in the atoms, is a necessary part of Life in the Universe. It is like the oxygen needed on Earth by all species. It is another reciprocal duty of the human with the Universe. This activation with positive energy, is that human activity historically interpreted by many cultures as the "adoration of the gods."

Upon further investigation, the X'Tolob discovered that the best manner of energizing the atoms, were dances/prayers/thoughts/songs directed at the Great Spirit. Specifically, prayers/thoughts/songs that promote Love. What could make more perfect sense, thought the X'Tolob? The Great Spirit is pure Love; and It has placed on humans the cosmic responsibility to express Love, so that the cosmic harmony can be maintained. After all these considerations, the X'Tolob concluded that the real purpose of thought, is to promote/express LOVE. They also concluded that LOVE is what sustains the Universe; without it, the Universe would cease to exist.

This understanding of the human role in the cosmic harmony, is the reason the ancestors used certain places within Mother Nature, to launch their dances/thoughts/prayers/songs to the Universe. These locations the X'Tolob and other learned teachers identified, contained concentrated energy that helped the dances, prayers, and songs, to achieve their intended objectives; of promoting Love for the Great Spirit, and all the spirits of Mother Nature. All the pyramids and temples the ancestors built, were on concentrated energy locations.

4

Chan, the Cosmic Serpents: In Lak'Ech

After centuries of deliberation and Panche Be investigations, the ancient X'Tolob had gathered enough information and knowledge to see the big picture of the Universe before them. They had investigated and confirmed many Truths accepted by their pueblos. Truths that were based on the science of Mother Nature that they had discovered. The X'Tolob did not conjecture; they painstakingly searched for the roots of all presumed Truths, using a methodical inquisitive scientific approach.

As they gathered more knowledge through their Science, the truths they found in turn became their Philosophy. Their Philosophy took the science of nature that they discovered, and used it to ponder the night sky, ask questions about a human lifetime, communicate with the magical spirit world, and create their mathematics. These were all interwoven with the science of Mother Nature that the X'Tolob discovered through their Panche Be investigations.

It was thus logical that this Science and the Philosophy that reflected the Science, would become the Worldview/Religion that the X'Tolob arrived at, and taught to their pueblos. Their Worldview was one where the human was an integral part of Mother Nature, living a reciprocal life with the animal and other kingdoms. Though an integral part, the human was not superior to any other forms of Life. Instead, all forms of Life were cooperators in the cosmic harmony. Being a cooperator in the cosmic harmony, meant recognizing that all forms of life on Earth live reciprocal lives, taking and giving while experiencing Life. Being a cooperator in the cosmic harmony, also meant that humans as cosmic beings have cosmic responsibilities.

In their search for expressing the necessity for cosmic harmony, the X'Tolob found the symbol that represented the entire experience of a human being. A symbol that represented many different facets of Life on Earth, as well as the potential to launch itself into the wonder of the night sky and the Universe. A symbol that represented Creative Energy within the Cosmic Consciousness. A symbol that would mathematically encapsulate the two magical numbers of the Mayan calendars: 4 and 13.

Once again, this symbol was the Serpent. The importance of the Serpent in Mayan history since ancient times cannot be overstated. This importance of the Serpent for the ancient X'Tolob was its *philosophical applications*, and *connection to evolution*. The Serpent's evolutionary importance for the Mayan nation, reveals itself in the ***"Popol Vuh"*** creation story. In this creation story, the human body was created from Corn, Water from the water serpent, and the "serpent's blood."

The Mayans writing the ***"Popul Vuh"*** with Latin characters in the 1600's used allegories/metaphors to convey their hidden meanings. In this creation myth of the human body, Corn represents the Earth, and Water (from the water serpent) is 98% of the human body. The "blood of the Serpent" is the life-giving energy/spirit from Father Sun that animates the human body. Thus, the human body is formed partially from the serpent of Mother Earth, and energized by the serpent of Father Sun.

Philosophically, to arrive at the symbol of the Serpent, the X'Tolob implemented MEN; and by Believing, they came to Create, and in creating, they Did. They encapsulated all the Scientific knowledge of their culture through their Philosophy (Believe), that allowed them to combine Science, Philosophy and the resultant Religion in a concept

(Create), that was expressed (Did) as the word KAN (pronounced Chan, meaning Serpent). In this expression, the exoteric meaning of CHAN was the same as the Absolute Being; since CHAN is both Circle (number 13) and Square (number 4), and the four elements; the same as Hunab K'u, the Great Spirit.

Knowledge, science, philosophy, history, legend, teach, learn, present, past, and future exist together and interwoven by CHAN the Cosmic Serpent, which represents them all while constantly transforming within the infinite Circle and Square of the Universe. In this philosophical manner, the Serpent became the supreme exoteric symbol of the Absolute Being; encompassing Existence since in the Serpent is also found the Plurality of Unity, geometry, and the mathematical numbers Circle (13) and Square (4).

NOTE: It follows logically that the various temples/depictions of the Serpent, as it later evolved into the Feathered Serpent, whether under the names of Quetzalcoatl, K'uukulcan, Gucumatz, and others; were numerous because they were really temples dedicated to the Great Spirit, which has no image.

Having established the symbol of the Serpent throughout their belief system, the X'Tolob gathered again to recollect all that their Panche Be investigations had revealed over the centuries.
They had come to recognize and understand the cycle of Life. They had determined that the Earth and all Life is the result of evolution that began with the four elements of Earth, Water, Fire, and Air. They had mathematically proven that the Great Spirit existed; and conceptualized the latent Seed of Existence, the Zero, as the starting calendar point of the Universe.

They had discovered the Creative Thought formula of MEN, which was the formula used by the Cosmic Consciousness to visualize and then activate Creation. They had confirmed that Mother Nature and all Life consists of complementary Dualities, including the soul and the spirit. They had confirmed all their Truths through the science of Mother Nature. They had created the first Bird Serpent Duality from Mother Earth and Father Sun and used this Duality as the first steppingstone to the cosmos.

Now they were ready to knock at the door of the Universe. For this cosmic move, the X'Tolob selected the best scholars amongst themselves, who adopted the name Chan. The Chan Serpents launched a Panche Be investigation in order to fulfill the task given them by the X'Tolob. Their task was to ascertain whether humans had cosmic duties beyond being cooperators in the cosmic harmony. **"What exactly entails being a cooperator in the cosmic harmony,"** they asked? They began their search for the roots of a possible Cosmic Duty Truth by exploring the Universe.

Through their dream world travels, the Chan became aware that there are multiple Universes existing side-by-side with each other. They were able to confirm this discovery by the existence of energy windows between the Universes. It was during their travels in this investigation that the Chan explored the so-called Thirteen Heavens and the Nine Underworlds of the spirit world, which followed the same evolutionary pattern of Life as on Earth. These are the Heavens and Underworlds where the consciousness/spirit evolves on its journey towards a new material human life.

The Chan investigation lasted several decades by Earth's time. Traveling throughout the vast Universe was exhausting, as truly there is no end to the Universe. Yet these travels also gave the Chan the opportunity to conduct thorough searches, and it was through these searches, that finally revealed the critical human Cosmic Duty the Chan hoped to find. This Cosmic Duty was already one humans have been expressing intuitively since the dawn of time, but without knowing its importance for the well-being and maintenance of the cosmos.

The Chan discovered that this Cosmic Duty was necessary for Life to exist and prosper throughout the Universe and the Thirteen Heavens and Nine Underworlds. Since the Heavens and Underworlds are spiritual, the evolution of Consciousness that occurs within them is dependent totally on the expression of this Cosmic Duty. This Cosmic Duty is literally the glue that holds all of Existence together in all the Universes, Heavens and Underworlds. This glue is LOVE.
This is the Cosmic Duty which depends on humans to express. Other species can certainly express Love in their own ways, but humans

are the only species which can energize harmonious atomic energies throughout the Universe through their expression of Love. Ceremonies, dances, poetry, songs and flowers are just part of the expression of Love. The Great Spirit requires, the Chan discovered, that Love be constantly expressed for the maintenance of the Cosmic Harmony.

Being the scholars that they were, and not used to dealing with emotions, the Chan pondered how to best express this Love the Universe demanded for harmony to exist. They were not satisfied with just accepting the existing expressions of Love their pueblos already practiced. They wanted to make Love an everyday and every moment experience. They wanted to find a GROUP LOVE. *"How could they achieve this?"* After much deliberation, during which they invoked the Cosmic Consciousness, the Chan arrived at the answer.

The answer was *"In Lak'Ech."* In the Yucatec Mayan language, *"In Lak'Ech"* means "You Are My Other Me." In creating this phrase, the Chan were relying on the Love humans have for themselves. Most persons, not all, love themselves. This love of the Self is what enables persons to have confidence in themselves and positively interact with others. By stating to other members of your family/community that you see them as a reflection of yourself, you are expressing your Self-Love, and now including them, to create a Group-Love. In doing so, for the Mayan philosophers, the "One" became the "Many."

Yes, once again, the hand of Duality was at work as the "One" transformed into the "Plural/Many," in the concept of *In Lak'Ech*. Practicing the concept of *In Lak'Ech* within your family was simple and almost automatic. When you included your community, the Group Love now spread like the ripples from a rock thrown into a lake.

Once that rock hits the water, little waves start spreading outwards in a circle around the point of impact. That is what happened with *In Lak'Ech*. Soon after you included your community as *In Lak'Ech*, it wasn't long before persons started expressing *In Lak'Ech*, to other pueblos beyond their own within the Mayan Nation.

But that circle of ripples, the Group Love, wouldn't be contained within the Mayan Nation. Over time, as Mayans encountered other Red Nations people, they expressed *In Lak'Ech* to them as well. By now, the Chan had been re-integrated into the X'Tolob again. The X'Tolob surveyed the impact and spreading influence of *In Lak'Ech* within humans and considered the logical next step in the evolution of *In Lak'Ech*.

"Aren't we humans part of Mother Nature? Aren't we humans related to all the other children/species of Mother Nature?" The simple answer was Yes. In this manner, the animal, fish, plant, mineral, bird, and insect kingdoms along with all other forms of life on Mother Earth, became *In Lak'Ech* as well. Everyone/everything was another version of oneself in this ever-expanding Group Love.

The philosophical logic was that Everyone/Everything, in spite of personal uniqueness within infinite Diversity, is another version of Oneself, because Everyone/Everything is the same Energy of the Great Spirit. *In Lak'Ech*. When they confirmed this Truth, it was logical for the X'Tolob to consider extending *In Lak'Ech* to the cosmos as well. In this manner, everyone/everything in the cosmos became *In Lak'Ech*. The stars, the solar systems, the constellations, the galaxies; all became another version of oneself. *In Lak'Ech*.

In this manner, In Lak'Ech became the Philosophy found through their Science and Religion that allowed the Maya to become a resident of the Cosmos. The Maya had launched themselves from Mother Earth and embraced their entire environment, the Universe. In this manner, the Mayan found his **Tamoanchan**, the home of the Feathered Serpent, the place where the harmonious balance of matter/spirit evolves freely, and in unison with the Great Spirit. The Mayan had become a cosmic being.

His integration into the cosmos was complete.

The Mexica Red Road

Esencia de las Cosas

Todo tiene su Medida y Movimiento
(Everything has a measured Life)
Que Tu Sol Sea Brillante...

Andres Segura Granados

Preface to the Mexica Red Road

The Yucatec Mayan Red Road conceived by the X'Tolob happened thousands of years ago. Over the succeeding centuries, the science of nature worldview of the X'Tolob was adopted and modified by many Red Nations pueblos. By the time the Spaniards appeared in the 1500's, the ancient Mayan knowledge and culture had been in decline for about 600 years. The X'Tolob were almost forgotten, as they had been succeeded by the H'Menes.

But not all of the ancient Mayan knowledge was lost. Before the arrival of the Spaniards, many centuries earlier, other pueblos like the *Teotihuacanos* and Toltecs had incorporated some of this knowledge. The Toltecs were a proto-Mayan pueblo that inherited the ancient X'Tolob knowledge and modified it into their own worldview. In the Mayan language, T'olt means to sculp, engrave, paint, work with stone, in other words, a craftsperson. The Toltecs left a legacy of having worked with stone for statutes, columns, spirits, and crafts. They may have spoken a variation of *Huasteca*, which is a bridge language between Nahuatl and Mayan, and which would have facilitated the knowledge transfer.

The Toltecs lived on the central Mexico plateau, and are believed to have conceptualized Ometeotl, Huitzilopochtli, and some of the eventual Nahua spiritual pantheon that was different from the Mayans. They did not conceptualize the Feathered Serpent, whose temple already existed in Teotihuacan 800 years earlier. The Toltecs likely re-named K'uukulcan as Quetzalcoatl. Some of the knowledge the Toltecs inherited and modified from the ancient Maya, and Teotihuacan, was in turn inherited by the Nahuatl-speaking Chichimeca.

The Chichimeca refers to the various tribes that inhabited Mexico's central plateau centuries after the Toltec civilization, who had occupied the same plateau, had disappeared. Martinez-Paredez believed that the Aztec Nation arrived amongst the Chichimecas around the year 1000. His belief is that the Aztecs learned and adopted Nahuatl from the Chichimecas, as there are numerous sources stating that the early arriving Aztecs amongst the Chichimeca spoke Nahuatl poorly. They also likely learned the Nahua spiritual pantheon developed by the Tolteca from the Chichimeca.

Regarding the origins of the Aztecs, there is no definite certainty as to the location of their origins, other than their oral tradition, which is that they came from Aztlan, the "lands to the north." The Aztec Nation would eventually consist of seven pueblos, once they settled into the Valley of Mexico. They were the Xochimilcas, Chalcas, Tepanecas, Acolhuas, Tlahuicas, Tlaxcaltecas, and other clans later to be known as the Mexica. They lived amongst the Chichimeca for at least a century, before journeying further south into the Valley of Mexico in the 1100's, but without the clans who had left earlier for the Yucatan, where they became the Mexica.

While living amongst the Chichimeca, the Aztecs learned not only Nahuatl but the philosophy/knowledge of the Toltecs that the Chichimeca had retained. Martinez Paredez relates that sometime in the 1100's, some Aztec clans appeared in the Yucatan. They were there in support of the Itza Mayan pueblo, which was battling another Mayan pueblo. The Aztec clans arrived wearing a red line on their faces, drawn from ear to ear. Below the red line was a glue that held feathers hanging upside down on their cheeks.

The ancient ***Tamoanchoas*** had conceptualized the Feathered Serpent thousands of years earlier, as we have seen, whom the Mayans called K'uukulcan in the Yucatec Mayan language. The Mayans immediately recognized this feathered Red Line on the faces of the visiting Aztecs as the adoration of the Feathered Serpent. The Feathered Serpent was known as Quetzalcoatl amongst these clans of Aztecs; a belief inherited from Teotihuacan tradition.

The feathered red line symbolizing adoration of the Feathered Serpent was the reason the Mayans called these clans of visiting Aztecs *"Meexikanoob,"* which in the Yucatec Mayan language, meant "bearded serpents." This was a declaration that the "bearded serpents" Aztecs were seen as followers/believers in the Feathered Serpent. Such was the use of symbolism amongst our ancestral relatives. In Nahuatl, *Meexikanoob* was translated as "Mexica."

These Aztecs now re-named Mexica had a somewhat glorious stay in the Yucatan for over a hundred years, including rebuilding and ruling Chichen Itza, under the leadership of H'Meex K'uuk, the serpent Mexica *tlatoani*. This is also the reason the Mexica did not accompany their fellow Aztecs when they left the Chichimeca in the late 1100's and moved down into the Valley of Mexico. The Mexica also built Mayapan as a new capital for the Yucatan. In the late 1200's, Hunac Creel of the Mayan Cocom pueblo defeated Chichen Itza, and this caused the Mexica to leave the Yucatan. This date also lines up with the late arrival of the Mexicas amongst their Aztec relatives, in the Valley of Mexico, to found Tenochtitlan in 1274-1325.

This history of the Mexica in the Yucatan was surprisingly confirmed upon reading Diego de Landa's *"Yucatan at the time of the Spanish Encounter. Chapters VI-IX,"* (2013). Diego de Landa was the bishop of Yucatan who burned every document/codex that he could find, besides viciously persecuting the Mayans, resulting in his being recalled to Spain and placed on trial for his actions. Perhaps in contrition, he thereafter published his account, or *"Relacion,"* of his times amongst the Mayas in the 1500's. The Mexica tlatoani mis-named Kukulkan was H'Meex K'uuk.

As their civilization grew and prospered in the Yucatan and later Tenochtitlan, the Mexica developed their own learned teachers, called the *tlamatinime*. The *tlamatinime* took the knowledge of the Toltecs and *Teotihuacanos* that they had learned from the Chichimeca and assimilated it with knowledge gathered from the H'menes of the Mayan Nation, while they were in the Yucatan. Together, the knowledge of the Toltecs, *Teotihuacanos*, and Mayans, were used to create their own Mexica worldview. The Mexica *tlamatinime* were learned scholars, like the X'Tolob, who took the same meticulous approach towards discovering their Truths. The path they took was to consider all Existence as the Energy of the Great Spirit, with infinite variations.

The Mexica energy worldview the *tlamatinime* visualized is what the maestro Andres Segura Granados called *"La Esencia de las Cosas."* This can be translated as "the Essence of Things." Philosophically, stating that you can define the essence of all Things, encompasses and denotes having knowledge of the entire Universe. This is a strong philosophical statement expressing confidence that your vision of the entire Universe is known and can be known. But not only a declaration that you actually Know the Universe, but understand its Essence, its components.

The *tlamatinime* pursued a vision of a world where Energy was everywhere, and the movement of energy in all cases could be manipulated and understood in a logical form. When I read the books of Carlos Castaneda in the 1960's, I thought them to be entertaining but fantastical when it came to describing the exploits of Don Juan, the Yaqui shaman. This was before my exposure to the Mexica worldview and my integration and understanding of it decades later.

Re-reading Castaneda recently, he makes total sense to me now. Don Juan wants to expose Castaneda to other ways of absorbing Life and experiencing other realities, than the limited Western worldview Castaneda comes from. A Western worldview limited to what one can see, feel, taste, smell, and touch. What he is describing in every book, is Don Juan's use of exercises to get Castaneda to visualize and understand transformations of energy, the manipulation of such, the existence of a heightened awareness, exploring the dream world, and communicating with the spirit world. These are all experiences intended to introduce Castaneda to a vision of Life beyond the limited Western view.

Don Juan arguably was a descendant of the Mexica *tlamatinime*; disciplined warriors studying the movement of energy and manipulating this energy in order to find the meaning to a cosmic life they envisioned. But they were true masters in comparison; Don Juan was a sorcerer, not a master. The *tlamatinime* pursued this worldview of understanding the movement and transformation of energy into the deepest reaches of the Cosmic Consciousness. This was a very different native worldview than that envisioned by the ancient Maya dreamers.

    Yet, the Mexica learned the lessons of Mother Nature, Duality, Tolerance, and the identity of being cosmic beings, from the Mayans. Using this knowledge as a base, the ***tlamatinime*** focused on how a lifetime impacts the journey of the eternal spirit, explored the "nuts and bolts" of the transformation of energy within Life, sought the interconnectivity of all energy and thus events, and formulated an organization/structure of the evolution of a human lifetime; all while using Universal Laws that applied to all Existence. In order to make observations/conclusions about a cosmic life, they sought to understand the effects on an eternal existence by the movement of energy. The Mexica worldview was thus the science of Energy.

    To make an analogy, picture Life as a giant plantation of Nature surrounding the Hacienda of Life. The Hacienda of Life represents a cosmic, eternal Existence. The Mayans were masters of all the Mother Nature surrounding the Hacienda; thoroughly integrating themselves with all the fauna and animal and other kingdoms that existed on the plantation lands. They had even knocked on the door of the Hacienda and quickly looked inside. The Mexica accepted all that the Mayans had learned/revealed about the lands and animal kingdoms. Their focus instead was on exploring thoroughly the insides of that Hacienda.

    The Mexica focused on exploring and understanding eternal life as they methodically searched the rooms of that Hacienda. They conceptualized and applied three Laws in their search for understanding the purpose of our current lifetimes within eternal time. These Laws were conceptualized to grasp/recognize how the Universe and Life has expressed itself since Creation. The first was the Law of Duality, which mandates that all energy manifests itself in dual form. This Law provided the needed structure to understand how Life unfolds in the Universe. The second was the Law of Causation, which connected all movements of energy relentlessly through succeeding lifetimes. The third was the Law of Compensation, which was a recognition that the Great Spirit has a Will that dictates supremely all movements of Energy and environment, in the Hacienda of Life.

1

The Mexica Red Road: Esencia de las Cosas

There is little known philosophy of the Aztecs/Mexicas before they lived amongst the Chichimeca. There is speculation that Aztec philosophy began, with the incorporation of the Toltec vision of the Great Spirit, from the Chichimeca. Since the Chichimeca spoke Nahuatl, the name of their Great Spirit was Ometeotl. This Nahuatl name means "Dual, or Two, God." The belief that Ometeotl originated with the Toltecs is just that, a belief without any known certainty. Since the legacy of the Toltecs was one of accomplishment, at least with stone, they are credited with conceptualizing Ometeotl and bequeathing this knowledge to the Chichimeca.

The description of Ometeotl is significantly different from the Mayan Great Spirit duality of Hunab K'u and Hunac K'u; and thus, we can conclude that the origins of Ometeotl are not Mayan. The name reflects that there are two components to Ometeotl. These two components of Ometeotl are positive and negative Energy, or male/female. Positive and negative are descriptive energy terms, not judgmental "good or bad."

In cosmic terms, the feminine negative half of Ometeotl that gives birth to all new Energy is *Omecihuatl*. Her male positive half which seeds this new Energy is *Ometecuhtli*. The two are thus complementary to each other, since they work as a Duality to produce Life. Because *Omecihuatl* serves as the "egg" of this energy Duality that produces Life, the Mexica Universe is necessarily matriarchal in its vision. This is the reason native societies trace their lineage through the mother.

This believed Toltec vision of Duality, was created by extrapolating to the cosmos, the examples of the unity of male and female which creates Life on Earth. If male and female create Life on Earth, and they do, then logically the female and male energies of Ometeotl creates Life in the Universe as well. The ***tlamatinime*** thus defined *Omecihuatl* and *Ometecuhtli* as the complementary energy halves of Ometeotl, the Life Source.

This vision of Ometeotl as the Cosmic Energy Duality expanded when the ***tlamatinime*** came in contact with the H'menes of the Yucatan. The Mayan vision of Duality was based on the structure of the Universe the Mayans had found through their mathematics, and Panche Be investigations. This Duality was the interaction of the "One" (individual), with the "Many" (group). The Mayan Duality, thus, was the expression of its twin, Diversity.

In Hunab K'u as the "One," and Hunac K'u as the "Many," the Maya expressed Duality as the all-encompassing, compassionate, interwoven, Diversity of the Great Spirit. This Mayan vision of Duality was confirmed by their mathematics and calendars. Whereas the Mayas recognized Energy as being the source of Hunab K'u and Hunac K'u, and thus, the Universe; they were more egalitarian, more harmonious, more humanity-oriented in their interpretations of the cosmic world than the Mexica. Perhaps the most valuable philosophical lesson the Mexica learned from the Mayans was Tolerance, through the recognition of Diversity.

Whereas the Mayans had taken centuries of generations of scholars to arrive at their worldview of unity with Nature, the Mexica sought to build upon this knowledge. They were more interested in the "nuts and bolts" of living a human lifetime. "Nuts and bolts" that considered the spiritual and the eternal in understanding the human experience. To accomplish this, they took a three-step process to create a framework for understanding the unfolding of Life in the Universe. The first step was to recognize Duality as the foundational structure of the Universe. The second step was to interweave all movements of energy caused by human choices, and their impact, and consider these from an eternal perspective. The third step was recognition of the preeminent role of the Great Spirit.

These steps were the Three Laws of Ometeotl. These are Laws that Ometeotl also follows, the *tlamatinime* believed, for there to be a consistency to the unfolding of Life in the Universe. These Laws govern both how the Universe is organized, as well as produce a framework, wherein the human can experience an interactive and reciprocal lifetime with the Great Spirit.   Thus, the Laws of Duality, Causation, and Compensation, were formulated to provide the understandable and responsible organization to the structure of the Universe the *tlamatinime* envisioned.

2

The Law of Duality

This is the first Law of Ometeotl and provides the structure of the Mexica Universe. This Law dictates/mandates that all Life in the Universe, all Existence, has a Twin. Always look for the other side, it will be there. Everything expresses itself in TWO forms. This elementary vision of Duality inherited from Nahua tradition was expanded when the Mayan vision of Duality was added. Expressed mathematically, the Mayan Duality was 1=2, and 2=1. That was the Mayan version of Duality, where the "One" and the "Many" resulted in the expression of Duality's twin, Diversity.

Since the Mexica were focused on energy, their vision of Duality was to explore Reality from the perspective of negative and positive energy interacting harmoniously with each other. This harmony was achieved because all the dualities of Life are complementary to each other. This Universal structure of complementary dualities is the simple explanation of the Law of Duality. But once you began to apply this Law to all Existence, it can become extremely complex.

It can become infinitely complex because the Law essentially dictates that the Universe also has a twin. Exponentially and mathematically, this means there are no limits to the sizes of the Universes. It also supports the belief that there are infinite parallel Universes existing side-by-side in the space of Existence. Such were the doors of possible Realities made available to our Mexica ancestors in applying the Law of Duality to their philosophical questions.

Continuing, the mathematical recognition of Duality formulated by the ancient X'Tolob was adopted by the *tlamatinime* and incorporated into the knowledge of Duality they had inherited from Nahua tradition. But being the warrior scholars that they were, they wanted to confirm Duality for themselves. They started by considering that the original Duality was composed of the negative energy of *Omecihuatl* and the positive energy of *Ometecuhtli*.

At the beginning of the Universe, *Omecihuatl* was the unconscious Cosmic Consciousness, the latent female egg of Creation-waiting-to-happen. The act of becoming conscious was provided by *Ometecuhtli*, who was the spark, the semen, that was needed to energize *Omecihuatl*. From this original Duality of Unconsciousness/Consciousness, the *tlamatinime* reasoned, all Life/Creation has flowed in consistent complementary Dualities ever since.

Up/down. How can you know something is up unless you know when it is down? *Here/there.* How do we know something is here unless we know when it is there? *Wet/dry.* How can we know the sensation of being wet unless we know the sensation of being dry? *Sick/healthy.* How do we know we're sick unless we know being healthy? The examples the *tlamatinime* encountered everywhere were consistently that of complementary Dualities:

Negative/positive. Subjective/objective. True/lie. Love/hate. Hot/cold. Inside/outside. Tall/short. Sweet/sour. Left/right. Fast/slow. Heavy/light. Clear/cloudy. Open/closed. Female/male. Balance/imbalance. Harmony/chaos.

These were all long-known truths amongst the pueblos. Everything has two sides, and can be viewed from multiple perspectives differently, depending on the interpretation of the viewer. This manner of observing Life was so ingrained in the pueblos, that few even gave Duality a thought or bothered to examine its role in Life.

But to examine and debate was exactly what the *tlamatinime* did in considering answers to their questions. They saw that just as the Universe had chosen to create planetary bodies in a consistent circular and elliptical form, the same Universe had chosen to express itself in Duality everywhere. These were the obvious objective truths the *tlamatinime* accepted as they now sought to harness the energy these Universal constants provided.

Once they confirmed Duality to be a Universal constant, the *tlamatinime* addressed the Life "nuts and bolts" issue of the duality of the Soul and the Spirit. For them, logically all forms had to have both a soul and a spirit, owing to the Law of Duality. This was a "nuts and bolts" issue because the soul and spirit were present everywhere in material Existence, and the preeminent example of the transformation of energy.

The soul was known/seen because the *tlamatinime*, who were master shamans, used their skills to visualize the energy of the various forms on Earth. The energy of every form manifests itself as an aura that envelopes the form. All material forms, like animals, fish, birds, insects, rocks, mountains, streams, clouds; have their own auras. The aura that surrounds the form was seen to be the soul of the form. The *tlamatinime* reasoned that since the components of all the material forms on Mother Earth come from her elements (Fire, Earth, Water, Air, Space), the energy of the Four Elements expresses itself as the soul of every form.

The spirit, on the other hand, comes from, and is part of, the Great Spirit, and animates all forms with the energy of consciousness. To animate means to give Life. In our solar system, this energy comes from our Father Sun, who serves as the agent of the Great Spirit. This is the role of Father Sun as the Feathered Serpent; the agent who provides the energy/spirit/consciousness from the Great Spirit that is needed to animate all forms of Life on Earth and give them the energy/spirit to have a conscious existence. The spirit thus serves as the consciousness of the form. While spirits serve as the consciousness of every form, they are pure energy, and thus have no form themselves.

The disposition of the soul and spirit upon "death" thus became crystal clear for the *tlamatinime*. Since the soul comes from the energy of Mother Earth, the cyclicity of Life mandates that it return to her once the form has died/transformed. For different reasons, not all souls are re-integrated with Mother Earth upon death and require other transformations. The reason all forms die is because its measured existence has ended, consistent with evolution and the cycle of Life, and its spirit has left the form and transitioned into the spirit world. Spirits, being part of the Great Spirit, never die, but are eternally transforming.

As they sought to understand fully the breadth of Duality, the *tlamatinime* considered its twin, Diversity. Diversity exists because *Omecihuatl* and *Ometecuhtli* mandate the constant creation of new Energy throughout the Universe. The new Energy constantly being created by the Duality of *Omecihuatl* and *Ometecuhtli* is necessarily diverse. It is necessarily diverse because Ometeotl is also constantly evolving, and the expressions of Life from Ometeotl change from milli-second to millisecond.

The world that existed while you read this sentence no longer exists, nor will it ever return. This constant evolution and change produce different infinite vibrational frequencies of Ometeotl's Energy. These different vibrational frequencies of Energy are what manifest themselves as the Diversity of Ometeotl. Diversity thus is responsible for the multiple variations of flowers, animals, humans, trees, insects, etc., that exist on Mother Earth. Recognition and acceptance of Diversity was very important because of the lessons taught by Diversity. The most important lesson Diversity taught was the lesson of Tolerance.

Diversity taught that all forms of Life on Mother Earth are related to each other, even though they are different from each other. Diversity taught that all organisms/life forms on Earth are also part of the cosmos. Diversity taught that humans are not superior to any other life form. Diversity taught that humans can be different in many forms, races, and sexes. Diversity taught that all viewpoints can be valid. Diversity taught differences in living a Life and experiencing a death. Diversity taught harmony. Diversity taught tolerance.

Tolerance is, the *tlamatinime* discovered, what "grows your consciousness." When a person realizes that humans are part of the

Universal family, without being superior to any other life form, and accepts and tolerates all the Diversity of their Earth family, one's consciousness will expand and grow in response to this recognition. ***Tolerance allows you to positively focus on yourself; instead of negatively diverting your consciousness to others.*** The knowledge and use of Tolerance denoted a transformation of the consciousness for the *tlamatinime*; a transformation consistent with Ometeotl's constant evolution and transformation.

Since their early deliberations, the *tlamatinime* had identified the process of transformation as manifesting the evolution of the spirit. Transformation occurs when you adapt to new information/knowledge and absorb it into your worldview. The importance of transformation was a major reason the Serpent was deemed to be the representative of such, for the Serpent faithfully sheds its skin (transforms) multiple times every year. In the human, the *tlamatinime* reasoned, this transformation occurs when the consciousness becomes aware of what it was previously unconscious of. This process of energizing the consciousness was called "growing your consciousness." As true warriors, they discovered that the most effective method to "grow your consciousness," was to be found within the Law of Causation.

3

The Law of Causation

The Law of Duality was conceptualized to organize and understand the structure of the Universe. The Law of Causation was conceptualized to interconnect all movements of energy within the Duality of Life. For the *tlamatinime*, the eternal evolution of the Universe was the primary source of all energy transformations. Within a human lifetime, human actions and choices are also transformations of energy. All these movements of energy were sought to be contained within an understandable Law of Causation.

Applying the Law of Duality to consider a human Life, the *tlamatinime* reasoned that there were two energy halves to a human lifetime. They concluded that Half of a human lifetime is determined by human actions/choices. The other Half of a human lifetime is determined by the Will of Ometeotl, or *la voluntad de Dios*. Ometeotl's Will was the genesis for the Law of Compensation. Both the Law of Causation and Compensation form the basis for the interactive relationship humans have with the Great Spirit.

In the human actions/choices HALF, the *tlamatinime* were seeking to clarify the issue of responsibility. As native societies had become more diversified and complex, the issue of responsibility was paramount in the minds of the *tlamatinime*. They wanted to understand who is responsible, when human actions interact with or impact, other humans and the environment. This organization of human actions/choices, and the movement of energy involved, was encapsulated under the Law of Causation. This Law connects all movements of energy, or actions, and makes individual actions accountable to the whole/group.

The first determination by the *tlamatinime* in this quest was defining human actions. ***"Can they be negligent without intent? Should all actions have consequences?"*** They started their search for answers to these questions by visualizing the Law of Causation as a giant web of Energy that encircles the entire Universe. Their conclusion that the Universe was circular was based on the recognition that the Universe *chose* to make all planetary bodies in a consistent circular form. A straight line was nowhere to be found anywhere in the Universe. The *tlamatinime* thus reasoned that it makes sense to consider Life and the Universe in the same circular form, with a cyclical movement.

What the Law of Causation does is connect all movements of energy within the circular web of Existence. Picture the Universe as a giant circular spider web which is constantly expanding. The web is composed entirely of vibrating Energy which ties everything together. This is the Energy of the Great Spirit. When anything happens on this web, it is because someone/something has moved energy. All movements of energy within the web are conscious, whether they are intentional or negligent. There can never be randomness or coincidence of any movement of energy on the web, since everything is the conscious Energy of the Great Spirit. Thus, there was no "wiggle-room" in the Law of Causation, to excuse/forgive any "unintended" movement of energy.

All movements of energy begun on the web of Life become a Cause, because it is the reason the movement of energy has occurred and is impacting other energy around it. The impact on others by the moved energy is known as the Effect. The Effect includes both the intended and negligent objects of the Cause. Because the web of Life is cyclical, all expenditures of energy will affect both the initiator (Cause) and the impacted (Effect) of that energy. This dual impact is called the "interconnectness of Existence," and is a major Rule of the Law of Causation. In this case, the Rule being that all energy returns to where it was first moved.

The value for the *tlamatinime* of the "interconnectness of Existence," is that it lay the foundations for how human actions interrelated together as Cause and Effect. The human is unique amongst the environment of Mother Earth, the *tlamatinime* concluded, because the actions of **all other life organisms are balanced and harmonious with Mother Nature. Only the human has the capacity to disrupt the cosmic harmony.** The *tlamatinime* were seeking to understand if all human movements of energy have consequences, since so many human actions have disruptive effects on the cosmic harmony. Again, the *tlamatinime* were searching for answers to the issue of responsibility within eternal lifetimes.

In their analysis, they started by considering the daily choices humans make. They recognized that daily choices are actions and therefore expenditures of energy. Thus, all choices, whether they be mental or physical, are movements of energy, which makes them a Cause. To visually understand how every Cause/choice will feel its Effect/impact, pick any point on a circle/globe. Trace your finger around that globe. Eventually, your finger will return to the point where it started. That is what is meant by saying that all Causes will feel their Effects. The point where the energy started, the Cause, will experience the energy it started, but now transformed by the impact it had on others, known as the Effect.

What the *tlamatinime* were seeking to understand was not the mundane everyday experiences of living, but the role of responsibility in making a choice that significantly impacted others. They concluded that those choices which benefit others creates good energy, and those which seek to harm others, creates bad energy. In either case, you either accumulate good or bad energy, based on the intent of the choices you initiate throughout your lifetime. It is the function of the Law of Causation to keep score on these lifetime choices you make, so that all energies "get paid." The maestro called this return of energy to you as ***"todo se paga"*** (everything gets paid). In modern terms, "payback" means the same thing.

Thus, you obviously want to feel the impact of good energy returning to you, rather than bad energy. You ensure good energy will return to you, by making choices which benefit others besides yourself. Should you make choices which are harmful to others, expect that you will experience this negative energy at some point in your future. Whatever type of energy returns to you, it is because "keeping score" of your actions is a basic function of the Law of Causation. Said another way, the Law of Causation does not forget nor forgive anything. For the *tlamatinime*, the Law of Causation was a relentless and faithful scorekeeper.

In "keeping score," the Law of Causation mandates that you will receive the Effect in a future lifetime, if you happen to die in your current lifetime, before the energy can return to you. This is how the "interconnectness of Existence" between material and spiritual existence transferred the movement of energy under the Law of Causation. It started with an understanding that the Energy which manifests as material, is the same Energy that comprises the spirit world. Thus, the consciousness/spirit of those humans who die without experiencing the Effect, takes this good/bad energy with them into the spirit world. Consciousness of this good/bad energy in the spirit world then transfers to your unconscious mind, which is your cumulative composite consciousness.

In exploring the energy connections between the material and the spirit world under the "interconnectness of Existence," the *tlamatinime* came face-to-face with reincarnation. After all, they recognized, reincarnation is also a movement of energy. In this case, the movement is the transition from spirit to matter. The *tlamatinime* knew that so-called death means your consciousness leaves your body and transforms into the spirit world. The spirit world shared that the spirit then undergoes a series of evolutionary changes before eventually manifesting itself again as a human. This knowledge allowed the tlamatinime to confirm that your consciousness is the eternal part of yourself, because consciousness is spirit, which never dies.

The *tlamatinime* concluded that reincarnation is mandated because the Great Spirit is constantly changing and evolving, and our spirits, being part of the Great Spirit, need to also constantly change and evolve as well. Mandated means reincarnation is not a choice.   Reincarnation made possible achieving the purpose of Life for the Mexica philosopher, which was to achieve re-integration with the Great Spirit. At some point in one of our future eternal lives, the *tlamatinime* reasoned, after you have experienced all human distinctions, and grown your consciousness in the process, you will be able to re-integrate with the Great Spirit. By achieving this reintegration, you will no longer require reincarnation, for you will be conscious of experiencing all the forms of Existence the Great Spirit does, without the need to experience another human lifetime. These were the beliefs of the *tlamatinime*.

Since the *tlamatinime* knew humans are one of the many organisms of Mother Nature, they pondered if reincarnation meant they might have future lifetimes as something other than human. The answer, they discovered, was no. It was NO because they had manifested in the Universe with the frequency vibration of a human, which was an assignment made by the Great Spirit. "Who are we," reasoned the *tlamatinime*, "to change or challenge the reasoning of the Great Spirit in having made us humans in the first place?" Their conclusion thus, was that humans will continue to reincarnate in the same human frequency.

Note: Here the Red Road is different than Buddhism and Hinduism, who believe reincarnation is possible in other forms than human.

In order to understand how spirit/consciousness interacted with the mandate of reincarnation, the *tlamatinime* considered the Law of Duality to conclude that a human has two consciousnesses. Your eternal consciousness is the cumulative composite consciousness of all your previous lifetimes. A cumulative consciousness means it is composed of all your previous personalities/consciousnesses from prior lifetimes. The cumulative consciousness is the consciousness which you will reexperience in the spirit world when your present lifetime ends. This cumulative consciousness is entrusted by the Law of Causation to take into consideration any accumulated good/bad energy of a previous lifetime and determine what needs to get paid/rewarded in the next lifetime.   In our human lifetimes, the cumulative consciousness acts as your unconscious mind.

*Note: Apparently, the renowned Swiss psychiatrist/psychoanalyst **Carl Jung** promoted his similar beliefs in this area of the conscious/unconscious, which mirror the Mexica view under reincarnation. He called the cumulative consciousness the "collective unconscious." He believed that consciousness doesn't appear until after human birth, whereas the Mexica believed consciousness expresses itself in the spirit world.*

The second consciousness is that of your present lifetime, the name/personality you identify as. This personal consciousness evolved from your eternal cumulative consciousness as part of the present lifetime. Because it is the personal consciousness which will experience the upcoming lifetime, this new consciousness has the responsibility to make its first choice of the Life yet to come. This choice is deciding the family and environment it will be born into. This choice is critical and places you into position to experience the kind of life you seek. In this manner, the *tlamatinime* taught, every one of us is responsible for having made the choice of our birth.

You alone are responsible, the *tlamatinime* educated, for having made the decision of the family and environment you are born into. Perhaps your spirit made the decision as the best manner to repay a mandated Effect from one or more prior lifetimes. Perhaps you wanted to experience Life again with other spirits you have previously shared lifetimes with. Perhaps you wanted to experience another human sexuality other than male/female. Perhaps you are attracted to another human culture and want to experience a life in that culture. Regardless of your reasons for making this choice, you and only you, made this choice for yourself. What the *tlamatinime* were emphatic about, was that you must not use the circumstances of your birth and resultant family, as reasons to complain about the challenges you now face.

That was the goal of the *tlamatinime*, as they searched deeper into the various aspects of Duality within the human experience. This understanding and acceptance of having made the choice of your birth circumstances is especially critical in those lifetimes where the person has serious disabilities, physical or mental. ***"Did the person choose such a difficult lifetime,"*** the *tlamatinime* asked? The Law of Causation answered firmly in the affirmative.

However difficult the choice must have been, given the resulting consequences, the spirit made the choice. It made the choice because the Law of Causation dictates a return of energy resulting from previous movements of energy, and the spirit determined that whatever disabilities were to be experienced in this upcoming lifetime, was the preferred method to receive the impact of the Law of Causation. Perhaps the knowledge of eternal lives yet to be lived, was a consideration for the spirit, in having made the choice it did for the disabled lifetime.

For the *tlamatinime*, making choices was a primary function of a human lifetime, because making choices is the method by which you interact with the Universe, and thus grow your consciousness. What the *tlamatinime* referred to as making choices, had to do with helping others, showing compassion and tolerance, expressing Love, being responsible for your actions, and being brave when needed. Or, making the choices of the opposite of all the above; never helping others, displaying no compassion and intolerance, refusing to take responsibility, and demonstrating cowardice in a time of need.

Whatever your choices may be, the Law of Causation dictates they will either become good karma, that can be used to give you a more fulfilling lifetime in this or a future lifetime, or bad karma, that will have to be paid now or in a future lifetime. There are no confessionals, nor dunks in the water, that can forgive under the Law of Causation. *Todo se paga.* In either case, **you are the one making the choice as to which version of Duality (good/bad) will manifest thereafter in your life by your actions**. The point being that all choices have consequences, because choices are movements of energy, and the Law of Causation mandates that the moved energy return to its origin.

Making choices allows you to have an interactive relationship with the Great Spirit and grow your consciousness at the same time. Making choices grows your consciousness because as you assimilate the consequences of your choices, this assimilation equals evolution, which makes your consciousness grow. The Mother Teresa that achieved what she did in her older age, was not the same Mother Teresa in her youth. The more she committed and helped others, the more her consciousness grew, and grew, until her death. The same Rule applies for everyone: the more tolerance and love you express, the more tolerance and Love that you will receive.

4

The Law of Compensation

Whereas Diversity is the twin of Duality, the Law of Compensation is the twin of the Law of Causation. The Law of Causation deals with human actions which are the choices we make and the consequences which those choices produce. The Law of Compensation, on the other hand, deals with the other HALF of Life, which is the Will of Ometeotl, or, *"la Voluntad de Dios."* This produced a worldview where half of a lifetime is dictated by your individual actions, and the other half by the Will of God. This once again describes the interactive relationship the native had with the Great Spirit.

Fortunately, the "Will of God," is the half of Life where all your actions/desires/wishes, are judged from the perspective of Love. The *tlamatinime* believed that the Great Spirit dispenses only Love; and the Love which is dispensed by the Great Spirit, is that Love which is for your greater good. The Law of Compensation, thus, is based on Faith that your interactive relationship with the Great Spirit will result in the **correct response** to your prayers/requests, regardless of whether such response is what you desire or not.

The *tlamatinime* conceptualized the Law of Compensation, with an analysis of how a human lifetime is interactive with the Great Spirit. They acknowledged that the human is the "wild card" of Life in the cosmic harmony, and human emotions can create a turbulent sea. The Law of Compensation faithfully provides a calmness that allows the human to navigate Life. In modern terms, it is literally an insurance policy that everything/Life will evolve for the greater good, both for the individual, as well as Existence.

The interaction begins with the human requesting something from the Great Spirit that the human desires. It could be a wished-for material gain, activity or employment, the attraction of a love, or the resolution of a problem in your favor. Requests include prayers, poems, songs, and thoughts, directed at the Great Spirit, with the intent that such request be granted.

The interaction develops because the Law of Compensation mandates that the Great Spirit MUST answer your prayer/request. As stated earlier, Ometeotl follows the same Laws as all other energy for the consistency needed amongst the ever-changing Universe. Since prayers/requests/thoughts essentially are movements of energy, directed towards the Great Spirit, the cyclical nature of the Universe mandates that the Cosmic Consciousness must answer these prayers/requests/songs.

When the Cosmic Consciousness of the Great Spirit responds, as it must, the answer always is Love, in one form or another. As in most emotions, Love can manifest in many different ways. Sometimes the answer of Love is Silence by the Great Spirit. Most often, silence means No. It is up to you, as the recipient of the answer from the Great Spirit, to determine the form of Love your answer manifests. While the answer may not at first impression seem to be Love, and is not what you hoped for, the Law of Compensation guarantees that the answer truly is Love, and for your greater good. Look for it, and you will find it. Have Faith in the Great Spirit.

The *tlamatinime* conceptualized and taught that the Great Spirit only promotes Love, never pain, intolerance, or anything harmful towards any part of Existence. Why? The analysis began with a recognition that the Great Spirit loves Itself. Because everything/everyone is part of the Great Spirit, why would It want to promote anything other than Love? Thus, when the Cosmic Consciousness of the Great Spirit answers your requests/prayers/thoughts, It will do so with your greater good in mind, because your greater good is It's Greater Good.

True to the Law of Duality, the answer of Love from the Great Spirit will come in one of two forms. When the answer is Yes, the Great Spirit has granted your request. From your perspective, you are happy with the Love the Great Spirit has shown and move on without giving it further thought. But when the answer is No, the likelihood is that you will be angry/disappointed. You may not appreciate or understand the Love the Great Spirit has shown by denying your request/prayer. This is when you need to internalize, in order to understand why the request was not granted. As you internalize, hopefully you will recognize why the request was not granted and understand that your request was not for your greater good, and you need to move on in Life.

What the *tlamatinime* determined by conceptualizing the Law of Compensation, and thereafter analyzing its application to human choices, became clear when they considered the role of Faith in the interactive relationship they visualized with the Great Spirit. A human being can withstand severe hunger, depravation, filth, and extreme danger, amongst other threats, if the human has Faith. Having Faith, and thus Hope, in the face of horrendous circumstances, is what oftentimes allows the human to continue to live her/his Life.

Faith, they discovered, is thus the reciprocal food humans give that nourishes the Great Spirit. In return for the cosmic nourishment the Great Spirit receives from the Faith of humans, the Great Spirit returns Love. This was another truth the *tlamatinime* discovered in their search for answers to the reasons a human lives a lifetime.

The *tlamatinime* developed a clear vision of their Great Spirit, Ometeotl, as the Energy/Life Force of Existence. They recognized a clear structure of the Universe which manifests itself in complementary Dualities. They conceptualized an understandable organization to this structure, consisting of the complementary halves of human actions under the Law of Causation, and the Great Spirit's response under the Law of Compensation.

Theirs was a measured approach to understanding the Universe and Life as pure energy. They were focused on how this energy can be manipulated and transformed and sought to understand the predictable consequences of all movements of energy. In their world, matter was merely energy in transition, energy that could be manipulated and made useful. Yet, the accumulation of matter for matter's sake had no cosmic purpose or benefit. All matter is temporary. What always mattered above all, was the growth of their eternal spirits. That was the Mexica warrior approach to Life.

Part Three

Decolonization

"Two centuries ago, a former European colony decided to catch up with Europe. It succeeded so well that the United States of America became a monster, in which the taints, the sickness and the inhumanity of Europe have grown to appalling dimensions"

...Frantz Fanon

1

Do Chicanos need to Decolonize?

The reader by now has a basic understanding of the Red Road. You have enough to distinguish how the beliefs of the Red Road worldview compare to the beliefs of your current worldview/religion. You now understand that walking on the Red Road **means you are conscious of everything that happens in your life every single moment of every day.**   This attention to Life is very different than the life white America extends, with its focus on the accumulation of material comforts, and sedating you with your favorite addiction before streaming media every night. If the exposure to the Red Road has made these differences starker, that is a positive sign that you are ready to consider whether you, as a Chicana/o/x, need to decolonize.

Until the mid-1900's, most of the people in the world were colonial subjects of the European countries. Africa, the Middle East, most of Asia except for Japan, Thailand and Korea, were all colonies or controlled by different European countries. All the countries of the Americas were/had also been colonies of the Europeans. The Europeans employed similar tactics and systems of governance in all their colonies, that had one consistent common feature. European control everywhere was grounded on the promotion of the superiority of Europe and white European culture. This promotion of white supremacy was enforced with military might.

White European, not all Caucasians. Europeans promoted that since they came from a superior culture, they were entitled to certain privileges that came with being white. For the European to control the majority non-white populations with this philosophy, they insisted that all their colonial subjects admit/believe that they, the subjects, came from an inferior culture. Admitting and believing that you, as a non-white person, come from an inferior culture, effectively identified you as a colonial subject. It also did nothing for the self-confidence of the colonized.

To gain that self-confidence, the colonized person needed to elevate their culture to at least the same level as the European.   The act of elevating their culture by colonial subjects began their de-colonization from any more beliefs in white supremacy and privilege. It took many decades, but with this elevation of native cultures worldwide, the European retreated and left his colonies.

Except for the Americas. Chicanos are thus distinguished, because we live in the "belly of the monster," and we cannot expect him to return to Europe. But, through decolonization, *we can erase the promoted validity* of his white supremacy arguments.

The first step of decolonization, by elevating your culture, starts with a recognition that your community comes from a legacy of being colonized. Thus, for Chicanos, decolonizing by elevating your culture means challenging the values/worldview of the gabacho, and rejecting his belief that it is superior to your own Mexican culture. We are discussing culture, not who has military or police power. Just as the human is not superior to any other life form, similarly, the European culture IS NOT superior to any other culture. Instead, all cultures are "equal cooperators in the drama of Life."

Given the present toxic environment of white supremacy in this country desiring to retain power, decolonization has become critical for Chicanos. The lid on the white racism that always existed has been removed by the anti-Christ aka 45 and his followers, and white supremacists are seemingly ready to take up arms to keep their perceived privileges. If Chicanos don't resist this blatant white racism, the black hole of white supremacy could usher in mass deportations or a return to Mexicans being relegated to field labor.

The analysis of a colonizer and colonized relationship was explained by Frantz Fanon in his classic, *"The Wretched of the Earth,"* 1961. Another excellent discussion of this relationship is *"The Colonizer and the Colonized,"* 1957, by Albert Memmi. Both essentially concluded that what the colonized person wants most desperately, is to resemble the white European colonizer. Both books explain that because the European colonizer's culture/worldview is deemed superior to that of the colonized, the colonized avoids darkening his skin, or seeks to lighten it, straightens/dyes one's hair, and lessens ethnic differences in facial/body makeup; all in order to look as much as possible like the white European colonizer.

The colonized celebrates the culture of the European colonizer (most federal holidays, St. Patrick's, Xmas, Thanksgiving, New Year's), equates being educated by how well you can communicate in English, and considers that whites should naturally be in positions of power. The colonized often suffers from **imposter syndrome**, which is to doubt your ability to compete with white people.

Given these examples, Chicanos should be able to conclude that most Mexicans fit the description of being colonized. Being colonized means most Mexicans still seek to gain mobility and meaning to their lives by adopting the values/worldview that the gabacho promotes. In doing so, they must navigate the gabacho's white supremacy and privilege society, by oftentimes becoming more *agabachado* (white) than the gabacho.

Fortunately for Chicanos, recent years have seen a tremendous increase in Chicanos moving towards examining their native roots. The dance circle amongst Chicanos/Mexicans now numbers in the thousands of *danzante* groups throughout the country. This trend towards a native identity amongst Chicanos, confirms that a significant de-colonization process is already happening within our community. The discussion that follows is intended for those Chicanos still struggling with beginning the process of de-colonization.

"Decolonization is the process of deconstructing colonial ideologies of the superiority and privilege of Western thought and culture." This is one of the better definitions of decolonization, and most certainly applies to any discussion of Mexicans/Chicanos and their relationship to Europeans. In our case, "Western thought and culture" means the same as European/Spanish/white American. In both Mexico and the United States, the European colonizer created colonies that promoted false histories/justifications that they are superior, and therefore entitled to the privileges they enjoy, simply because they are white.

For those Chicanos seeking decolonization from this mentality of white superiority, **the Red Road offers a cosmic alternative**. This book's approach towards the subject of decolonization for the Chicano shall take the same objective-seeking methodology of our Mayan ancestors. This is the Panche Be approach, where we will seek to objectively consider those values (roots) that the European has brought to our mestizo tree. We are not interested in demonizing either the Spanish or the white American worldviews. Spaniard or gachupine, and gringo/white American/gabacho, are used interchangeably as descriptive names, and not meant to be derogatory, but rather, "Chicano expression."

In considering both objectively, we must know the true history of events in Mexico and the United States, and not just the European versions. Only by knowing the truth of how the Europeans came to rule in the Americas, can we determine if we wish to retain any values from either. Thus, we will explore the roots and effects of European colonization in Mexico and the United States, in order to assess the truth of the need to decolonize ourselves from them.

For our Panche Be methodology, we shall borrow from our Chinese relatives in searching for the roots of the truth. The long-term value of traditional Chinese medicine involves the boiling of herbs, insects, and tree barks in water, until the water reduces and turns to a dark mud. You drink this dark foul-tasting mud because your internal organs are thanking you for the nourishment/healing they are receiving.

The true history of the European is what we shall uncover during our Panche Be search, using the Chinese method. It may be a brutal medicinal truth, as brutal as the Chinese mud, but this truth will have the same effect: nourishment/healing, in this case, for our brains and consciousness. Again, we are not about demonization; we are about searching for the truth so that we can use this truth to illuminate and guide our path on the journey of Life.

For a mestizo, the definition of what you are, is the result of the colonization by the European in Mexico. Spain imposed a racial system on their colony of New Spain which mandated that all races were subject to Spanish control as colonial subjects. At the top of this racial system was the Spaniard born in Spain, followed by the Spaniard born in New Spain (the Americas). These persons were the only ones who had power, wealth, and influence within the colony. More specifically, of course, the benefits of this society were in the hands of Spanish men. Yet the Spanish woman was above all the mestizos, mulattos, and Indians in this race-based society.

Mestizos were the direct product of the colonial interaction between the Spanish man and the Indian woman. "Colonial interaction" is a kind term, because in the overwhelming number of early cases that produced the mestizo, the Indian woman submitted as the slave/servant to the Spanish master. Mulattos had the same heritage, the African slave submitting to the Spanish master. With time, mestizos and mulattos also mixed. Regardless, unless your Mexican ancestors were pure-blooded Spaniards, they were colonial subjects.

When the Mexican crosses the border into the United States, does her/his colonial status continue? Yes, the colonial status of being Mexican continues in this country. The only difference is that the dominant European worldview is now exchanged from the Spanish-based system to the white American. Once again, the promotion of white supremacy and privilege continues, this time under the dominant culture of white America. The culture/mongrel status of the Mexican is considered inferior/subservient, because he is part-Indian. Only the very light Mexican has any mobility, because he passes for being white. The racial politics of the United States is another form of control by the colonizer, similar to what the Spanish employed by their race-based system.

The gringo employs his race-based system which justifies ignoring the theft of all lands and the mass murder of Native Americans, the enslavement of the African, and the promotion of a false Manifest Destiny. Both the Democrats and the Republicans have adopted these false histories and narratives. All these false histories and more were justified since the religion of the white American promoted a "God given right" to white supremacy and privilege. Thus, the Chicano seeking to decolonize from his colonial status, must deconstruct both European legacies of the Spaniard and the gringo.

Returning to the definition of Decolonization, "deconstructing" means the opposite of building something. When you deconstruct, you are taking it apart piece by piece. This means you weigh/consider the value of the different components you are examining, and then you get rid of those components you don't want. Of course, in order to deconstruct anything, you must know the components that were used to construct them in the first place. An example of effective deconstruction regarding the gringo, as will be shown, is to flush away his white supremacy and privilege arguments, while embracing his ideals for democracy.

Continuing, "colonial ideologies" is much easier to understand. In the case of Chicanos/Mexicans, the colonial ideologies pertinent are the Spanish and the white American. "Colonial ideology" means the worldview promoted by the dominant culture, in order to justify minimizing the perceived inferior culture, of the colonized persons of the society. Both the Spaniards and the white Americans came from Europe with a worldview that they were superior to all other races and therefore entitled to white privilege. Even though Mexico officially gained its independence from Spain in 1821, the Spanish white supremacy worldview has continued to dominate Mexican society to the present day. This, in the face that most of the recent Presidents of Mexico since the Revolution have been mestizo.

Chicanos have been impacted by this Spanish version as well, even though we were born/raised in the United States. We are impacted because regardless of the number of generations our families have been here, we belong to a community which is composed of continually immigrating Mexicans, whose culture and worldview continues to be integrated into our own. What they have brought from Mexico has been the status of being mentally and economically colonized to the Spanish version of white supremacy and privilege. Once the Mexican crosses the border, history has shown that his colonial mentality compliantly trades the Spanish version and accepts the white American version instead.

"The superiority and privilege of Western thought and culture" is the description of what the European has promoted throughout the world. It means exactly as it reads: that in both Mexico, and the United States, the European has created false histories to promote their narrative that they come from a superior culture than that of the native cultures. For the European, a superior culture that produces superior thought. Furthermore, that what they did in gaining that superiority, was justified by what they contributed to the lands they came to govern.

Both their false histories and justifications are driven by a promotion of Western thought and philosophy, which the European claims is superior to the thought of nonwhite cultures. In fact, the thought of non-white cultures is either ignored or demonized. This all equals, in their eyes, to an entitlement to their white privilege. The following analyses are necessarily brief and to the point. Exceptions can certainly be found, but in general the conclusions are objectively valid.

2

Deconstructing the Spanish colonial legacy

Chicanos can begin the deconstruction of their colonial DNA by understanding how that DNA was impacted by historical events in the motherland of Mexico. Regardless of how many generations your family has been in the United States, even before Mexico was Mexico, your ancestors at some point after 1519, came from Mexico. Obviously, those of you with many generations here have been less impacted by the Mexican DNA than those of us, like myself, that were raised by Mexican *campesinos* who came to work and settled here during and after *la Revolucion*. Then there are the most recent immigrating members of our community, regardless of their so-called legal status. The recent Mexicans and Central Americans coming are more likely to be indigenous, rather than mestizo. This status of being indigenous adds more chile into our salsa.

This brings up an important distinction between Abya Yala natives, and immigrants coming to this country from elsewhere in the world. We are native to this hemisphere. Members of our ancestral original pueblos (clans) have been coming and going between different pueblos for thousands of years. This movement of energy/culture is the lifeblood of Abya Yala (the Americas). It therefore behooves all identities of Mexican to consider the colonial legacy which we have inherited from Mexico.

In the colonial Spanish version that began in 1519, the imposed colonial ideology was built on the race of the individual. "Peninsular Spaniards" born in Spain were superior to all others in the colony of New Spain. They were even superior to the "creole Spaniards" born in the Americas. In turn, not only were both Spaniards superior to all others, their culture and religion was enforced as superior to any existing native Indian beliefs/culture. It was enforced as being superior by mandating that all original pueblo cultures be considered inferior, and native religion eliminated.

Before we proceed to examine the white supremacy system the Spaniard installed in the Americas, let's consider who this Spaniard was. There were essentially two types of Spaniards who came to promote their agendas. One was the "conquistador," the military adventurer who came to acquire property, make money, and live lavishly on the labor of his slaves. Early on, his only god was acquiring gold and wealth, but he did answer to the King and, to some degree, the Catholic Church.

The other type of Spaniard came with the pious robes of the priest, seeking to expand his religion. This religion was 40 years into terrorizing their own population with the Spanish Inquisition, which justified the indiscriminate killing of Jews, Moors, and Protestants, along with the obligatory "witches." The Spain of their time had just re-gained control of all lands after 800 years under Moorish rule. It was recently ruled by an extremist Catholic zealot who promoted the Inquisition, *Isabel la catolica*. By any standards, both types of Spaniards were themselves extreme zealots in the pursuit of their goals.

But in order to truly deconstruct what the Spaniard represented to our native ancestors; we must take the time to dig deeper. The Spaniard of the 1500's, quite simply, was a horrible human being. These were the two extremist versions of humanity the Spaniard brought with him to New Spain: a cruel, greedy, and militaristic adventurer without any sense of human decency, and a pious hypocritical promoter, of a corrupt/fanatical version of a religion, seeking to fight the growing Protestant threat in Europe.

To the trusting natives who believed in harmony and respect for all Life, both Spaniards were like hungry wolves turned loose in the sheep's pen. Both versions of the Spaniard had no understanding of/interest in, what it meant to be living a reciprocal lifetime, with the natural and animal kingdoms. Neither Spaniard had beliefs that approximated a cosmic identity with cosmic purpose. Neither Spaniard understood a flow to Life. Instead, they were motivated by a materialistic worldview and a religion that promoted individual and Church gains at the expense of the many/downtrodden.

This extreme nature of the invader expressed itself early on, when the Spaniard insisted that native culture in all forms be considered inferior, and not worthy of intellectual consideration. If the Spaniard was willing to burn/torture his own people, and he was, this was the same horrible human now more than willing to burn/torture the Indian. Both Spaniards actively sought to destroy and eliminate the native Indian culture, and especially any leaders. The point being that in the Spaniard, the original pueblos encountered a human being who acted totally outside the norms of any known native civilized conduct. The Spaniard lied, cheated, betrayed, lashed out cruelly; all without remorse, shame, or justification.

The conquistador insisted that the Indian become compliant colonized subjects, literally slaves under constant threat of death. Meanwhile, the Spanish priests sought to "de-Indianize" the natives by denigrating their culture, civilization, and religion. The priests forced the children of the Indian "elite" into schools with the express purpose of turning these students into Christians. There, the children were "educated" into becoming promoters of the Spanish white supremacy and privilege ideology to their own people.

The mestizo, and to a lesser extent the mulatto, had more opportunities under this racist society than the Indian. But in order to realize any gain, he had to honor as superior the Spaniard's culture, religion, and authority. He had to deny his Indian/African heritage and culture, and instead adopt as superior the white European's religion and culture. To institutionalize matters, the Spaniards utilized a "divide and conquer" strategy, by making mobility within the society dependent on how much Spanish blood one might have.

The amount of Spanish blood was measured by how you looked. There were countless examples of siblings, some light with greater mobility, and their darker siblings with less mobility. At the base of this racial society were the Indians, which meant they had no mobility. Under this society, there was little motivation for the mestizo, especially the lighter ones, to identify with or learn about her/his native ancestry.

This racially imposed lack of motivation for the mestizo to know his Indian half, is the basis for the solitude/emptiness in the mestizo's soul, as described by Octavio Paz in his classic, *"The Labyrinth of Solitude,"* (1950). In most early cases, this lack of opportunity was not the choice of the mestizo, but rather was mandated by the mestizo's father, the gachupine, who likely produced the mestizo by raping his Indian mother.

She was in no position to attempt a return to her pueblo when her gachupine master forbade her any such choice. Or perhaps her mestizo child may have been rejected by her pueblo? **But that was 500 years ago, why hasn't the mestizo in Mexico discovered the cure for Paz' solitude?** It seems obvious for a Mexican mestizo, that what was difficult before, knowing one's native half; is at hand at any time, in today's Mexico. The mestizo lives alongside the original pueblos, yet seems to ignore their existence, as his eyes have 20/20 vision only for Europe. The mestizo just has to make the effort.

Had the mestizo been able to learn their native history 500 years ago, they would have discovered a very different native approach to territorial expansion before the coming of the European. In his book titled *"Mexico Profundo: Reclaiming a Civilization"* (1996), Guillermo Bonfil Battala points out that the primary purpose of expansion by the Aztec Triple Alliance was to obtain tribute from the defeated pueblos. The Triple Alliance was composed of the Mexicas leading the Acolhuas and Tepanecas; all Aztecs. The tribute to be paid to the Triple Alliance was whatever the defeated pueblo was already growing or producing. Tribute could also be paid by military or administrative service.

Because both the Triple Alliance as well as the defeated pueblos were from the Red Nations, there was no pressure on the defeated pueblos to accept the Mexica religious or philosophical worldview. To the contrary, it was not uncommon for the Mexicas to integrate part of a defeated pueblo's vision of the Great Spirit into their own beliefs. In many cases the spirit being honored was the same, only the name changed from pueblo to pueblo, as in the case of Tlaloc and Quetzalcoatl amongst the Nahua, and Chac and K'uukulcan amongst the Maya.

The Mexica also tolerated the defeated pueblo's form of governance as well as its language, meaning the defeated kept ruling themselves subject to Mexica oversight. On the subject of human sacrifice, this was the ritual "War of Flowers," where whoever pueblo lost would become honored sacrifices for the needed cosmic order and harmony. In essence, the main imposition to any defeated pueblos, before the coming of the Spaniard, was having to pay a form of tribute to the Mexicas.

When the foreign Spaniard arrived with his cunning and murderous worldview in 1519, using his superior military weapons and pious Bible, subjugation to his cruelty and lack of morality **was like now living in another Universe**. The native worldview of harmony with Mother Nature was deemed not only inferior, but illegal and unwanted. Catholic doctrine preaching the superiority of the European was crammed down the Indian throat, with those resisting paying the penalty of death. The languages of the defeated pueblos were discouraged and punished for being spoken, a practice that Mexican schools still employ in the present day to force the sole use of the foreign Spanish in their schools.

The Spaniards wanted more than tribute from the defeated Indians. They wanted Indian labor to mine for gold and other minerals they lusted after, labor to expand cattle and other meat-producing enterprises, labor to pursue other industries, including the deforestation and sale of trees, that were new to the Indians, but desired by the Spaniards. In other words, the Spaniards mandated that the traditional life of all the original pueblos, was to be totally altered in order to pursue and satisfy, what the Spaniard sought/dictated instead.

Common sense tells us that all the above actions the Spaniards took, caused a dramatic, sometimes fatal, trauma upon our native ancestor's minds and personalities. They went from being free human beings with a harmonious worldview to literally being molded into robotic slaves whose worldview was deemed inferior and demonic. The differences between being subjugated by the Mexica, versus sustaining the annihilation of your entire worldview and humanity by the Spaniards, cannot be overstated.

It was the total intent of the Spaniard to blot out any "nativeness" from all Indians and replace the unwanted culture with a compliant version of a human robot doing the bidding of his new Spanish master. That mental trauma of forced resignation to being deemed inferior, would filter down throughout the DNA of the original pueblos' generations for at least 300 years. Compliant mestizos have done little since 1821 to relieve this mental and cultural trauma our original pueblos continue to experience. Yet, the original pueblos persist.

Of course, there was no continuation of the pueblo's traditional governance under the Spaniards. Old leadership and structure were thrown out or murdered and replaced with compliant Indians instead. There was only one law and government in New Spain, and the Indian wasn't invited. The languages and cultures of the pueblos were discouraged and actively destroyed in many cases.

Shall we add that the Spaniards killed/infected/worked to death, millions of Indians in the first decades of the occupation? Should any argument be heard that the Spanish atrocities were somehow justified because the *"Aztecs did the same thing,"* you will know that white supremacy and privilege is rearing its ugly head once again with another false equivalency. The Aztecs/Mexicas never came close to doing what the gachupine did, and continues doing, through his descendants today, in subjugating people.

To put the Spanish racial system in another context, the genocide Nazi Germany did, was minimal compared to what the Spaniards did to the original pueblos. The numbers speak for themselves: six million Jews versus 56 million Indians. Shall we add that there were Jewish conquistadores, the conversos/marranos, who came with Cortez? This extreme practice of white supremacy and privilege existed for approximately 300 years until Mexican independence in 1821.

Bonfil Batalla argues that two Mexicos have existed since, one imaginary and one real. The Mexico of the *blancos* and of the power-sharing mestizos is what he calls the "imaginary Mexico." This is the Mexico romantically promoted to the world in history books and in today's movies and streaming media. This is a Mexico which constantly seeks re-assurance from Europe for its culture, religion, and finance. This imaginary Mexico paints its original pueblo citizens as those whose only value to the country is as objects of tourism. Otherwise, for them, all the original pueblos have forgettable pasts.

The "imaginary Mexico" sometimes paints itself as the land of the *norteño*, with sombrero (now replaced with cowboy hat), boots, and scarf around the neck, of course; as well as the resorts of Puerto Vallarta and Cancun, amongst others. It is the imaginary Mexico one sees in the business *centro* of the CDMX, or perhaps San Angel, Coyoacan, Roma, and other upscale neighborhoods. Outside of Mexico City, the imaginary Mexico can also be found in select neighborhoods of Monterrey, Puebla, Guadalajara, Culiacan, San Miguel Allende, and the like. Members of this white/light skinned imaginary Mexico, are also the lead actors/actresses for the television novelas, movies, and other media seen throughout the country and abroad. They also populate the billboards and advertisements on city buses.

The **"*Mexico profundo*"** (real Mexico), on the other hand, constitutes all the original pueblos and the overwhelming majority of mestizos and mulattos in the country. In the CDMX, the Mexicans of the **"*Mexico profundo*"** are the bus and uber drivers, restaurant workers, nannies, market vendors, and the darker people who live outside of the gentrified neighborhoods. The metro and the overcrowded buses are the transportation choice for these Mexican ***profundos***, because they are the least expensive. The ***profundos*** eat regularly throughout the day from *taqueros* and *mercado puestos* as opposed to sit-down restaurants. The **"*Mexico profundo*"** Mexicans are the inhabitants of Tepito and the other *colonias* and towns that surround Mexico City.

In the countryside, *"Mexico profundo"* expresses itself in the campesino, regardless of the racial mixture, and most mestizos/mulattos throughout Mexico. Of course, all the original pueblos from throughout the entire country are also members of the *"Mexico profundo."* Poverty and lack of opportunity is a common denominator for a member of the "Mexico profundo." Bonfil Batalla argues that most of the mestizos/mulattos are indistinguishable from the original pueblos, since they occupy the same lower strata of the economy, and most have retained and incorporated important parts of original pueblo culture within their communities.

However, since the "imaginary Mexico" controls Mexican society, the *"Mexico profundo"* members constitute the larger darker background that rarely gets any media coverage or analysis. The *"Mexico profundo,"* especially the Indian portion of this population, had never had an Ethnic Studies or such in the 500 years since *la Conquista* to learn about themselves in any academic format. The "imaginary" Mexico still insists that all public education be in Spanish, ignoring the reality that perhaps 90% or more of the original pueblo students speak their own native language. Until recently, any education these native *profundos* received ended in the 6th grade, and totally ignored the original pueblos' cultures and contributions.

Finally, in 2018, a new agency which will hopefully give the original pueblos an opportunity to define themselves, was begun under the initials INPI (National Institute of Indigenous Pueblos). This was created under Lopez Obrador, the current President of Mexico. It literally took 500 years for the original pueblos of Mexico to finally have an agency dedicated to improving their living and educational opportunities. Also included under the INPI umbrella are the Afro-Mexicans, who have been historically neglected for 500 years as well.

For Chicanos seeking to de-colonize, reading Bonfil Batalla will give you the insight needed to better understand the environment in Mexico our abuelos/padres emigrated from. This environment still exists today, continuing to influence the minds of Mexicans coming to the United States, contributing to the willing transfer of their colonial consciousness from the Spanish version to the gringo version. By understanding the societal structure of Mexico to the present day, Chicanos will be able to recognize the differences between the mestizo of Mexico and the Chicano of the United States.

Mestizos in Mexico are still mainly promoting Europe and its values while hardly, if at all, considering the treasure of native knowledge available to them, especially considering that the original pueblo communities exist all around them. In other words, the mestizos of Mexico are similar to the Mexican Americans, in that both seek upward mobility within their societies by honoring the colonial umbrella of white supremacy and privilege.

Is it any surprise, thus, that the Mexican community of this country historically are ***"profundos"*** who came North? They came north with low expectations, and a willingness to provide the manual labor, the gringo needed to develop the lands of the Southwest. Conservatively, probably 95% of all Mexicans who came to this country were from the ***"profundo"*** portion of the Mexico population. This colonial legacy of being from the ***"profundos"*** is one reason it took decades for later generations of Mexican immigrants to finally focus on education and societal involvement. Compare our history in the US with that of more recent immigrants from other parts of the world: the Indians, Pakistanis, Arabs, and others, who have sent many educated and aspirational members to this country and whose children are now professionals.

The above is a short recitation of the colonial legacy Chicanos have inherited from their Mexican ancestors. It is necessarily very basic with broad generalities, yet it is also brutally truthful. While the Spanish racial system is no longer officially operating in Mexico, in practice, this racial system continues to dominate today's Mexico. It is indisputable in Mexican society that white, Jewish, and Middle East/Asian Mexicans, have greater mobility than mestizos; whose lighter members have greater mobility than the darker mestizos or mulattos, with the original pueblos continuing to have very little mobility.

The Mexican mestizo continues to look towards Europe while largely ignoring the tremendous brain power and cultural treasure the original pueblos can contribute to the modern nation. Having traveled extensively throughout Mexico since 1968, I have seen very little interest by mestizos in regards their native ancestry. The Chicana/o cannot expect to receive any help from the Mexican mestizo, and thus must look internally to deconstruct the Spanish legacy of white supremacy and privilege.

Why is there such a difference regarding our native ancestors, between the Chicano and the Mexican mestizo? The Mexican mestizo utilizes what he perceives to be his native language, Spanish, and his only cultural conflict seems to be choosing between Spain and some other European country. The hundreds of original pueblos with their languages, culture, and history, that surround him; seem to be of no interest to him. The Mexican mestizo, in effect, has not developed his consciousness beyond the adoration of the European. He remains a colonized subject.

The Chicano, on the other hand, recognizes that Spanish is a foreign language, even though he may use it for his benefit. The Chicano is not interested in idolizing this foreign Spanish language while he navigates existence amongst a foreign cultural society, the gringo, who speaks another foreign language, English. The **Chicano is thus a double colonial.** In the analysis of de-colonizing and rejecting the gringo, the Chicano also rejects the Spaniard; for both are European. For the Chicano, rejection of our European heritage leaves our native ancestry as the roots, which we choose to grow our family trees with. Therein is the difference between the Chicano and the Mexican mestizo.

We have enough history from the above to begin the deconstruction part of this Spanish colonial legacy. We now know the components of this legacy we need to deconstruct. We have done that by discussing how events shaped/distorted the colonial Mexican mind since 1519. We have seen how the Spanish conquest forced a total re-definition of the purpose, religion, and culture of the original pueblos. We have discussed the brutality of the racial system the Spaniards installed to promote white supremacy and privilege, and to control their colonial subjects.

We have considered the fanatical Catholicism the Spanish priests imposed upon the original pueblos. In the process, the priests destroyed all objects of native worship, and actively promoted the demonization of native values in the minds of the original pueblos. The same Spanish racial system continues to impact most mestizos, Afro-Mexicans, and the original pueblos today. We have considered the reality that two Mexicos really exist: the "imaginary" and the "real" Mexico.

Chicanos do not live in that society where the Spanish legacy continues. But some recent members of our community still arrive with the Spanish legacy ingrained in their minds, and their interaction with Chicanos affects all of us. Consider the example of a young woman who recently immigrated from an original pueblo of Oaxaca, was admitted into a university courtesy of Chicano efforts, majored in Chicano Studies; yet afterwards, criticized Chicanos (read mestizos) for having violated her community and culture! The young woman was still obviously traumatized by the Spanish legacy alive in Mexico and has been slow to develop her consciousness that there are significant differences between the mestizo of Mexico and the Chicano of the United States.

The major deconstruction for Chicanos of the Spanish legacy, ***is simply not to glorify anything Spanish***. After all, the Spaniard plays the role of the rapist in our family drama. Not only the rapist, but a brutal rapist and cruel murderer as well. Why would Chicanos want to glorify anything this rapist/murderer contributed to our family tree? I'm not advocating forgetting Spanish if you know it. It is a convenient tool to communicate with Mexico, Latin America, and Spain, and for that reason, is worth keeping after deconstruction. Just don't glorify the language simply because it is the language colonial Mexicans speak, as opposed to the English of the gringo.   They are both European languages, and we want to de-colonize from the Europeans.

That is the critical component needed to de-colonize yourself from the Spanish legacy: to stop glorifying or honoring ANYTHING that promotes the Spaniard. This colonizer has never made any effort to recognize the murderous actions and cultural destruction he brought to the original pueblos. If this colonizer isn't interested in reaching out to us, why should we honor him and his culture in any manner whatsoever? Mexico has demanded an apology from Spain, and Spain's answer is to ignore Mexico. Spain's obstinate refusal to consider their inhumanity and the rape of their former colonies deserves derision and repugnance.

The lasting legacy of the Spaniards, besides their language, is their religion, Catholicism. More recently, some evangelical forms of Christianity are part of the legacy Chicanos have inherited from Mexico. We shall examine this religious portion of the legacy below, since whatever religion the Chicano practices, is done in the United States.

3

Deconstructing the gringo colonial legacy

This is the critical deconstruction Chicanos need to focus on in order to decolonize themselves. This should be obvious, for we live in the United States, and the white supremacy system here is different than the Spanish version our ancestors left in Mexico. The gringowear they give Mexicans/Chicanos to "join America," comes at a big price. The price is accepting the gringo's vision of his "God-given right" to supremacy and subsequent entitlement to privilege.

A gringo vision of white supremacy and privilege, not that dissimilar from the Spanish version, except that this European came from northern Europe. A vision that describes the Earth as a planetary rock without a life of its own, and a consistent source of potential income. A vision that sees Nature as an enemy that needs to be defeated, and that can be raped and violated at will. A vison that justifies all that the white man does in his pursuit of accumulating more material wealth and perceived power, because his religion promotes that God has so sanctioned his "right to supremacy and privilege." This is the price Chicanos/Mexicans have paid to live in the United States.

The earliest European settlers were from England and northern Europe, and they were essentially unwanted by their home countries. They were unwanted because they belonged to different sects of extreme Protestantism, whose religious interpretations of the Bible were against the prevailing and majority beliefs of more moderate Protestants. The leading theologian for the extremist Protestants was John Calvin. Calvin preached that God had predestined, before a human is born, who will be "saved or damned."

Who interpreted what God had predetermined? The Calvinists believed that every reverend, regardless of education or preparation, who had a congregation, was free to interpret the Bible and proclaim that his interpretation was "a revelation from God," and therefore legitimate. This belief is called predestination, which essentially means that before you are born, God has already determined if you will be "saved," or "damned." Conveniently for the Calvinists, **they were the ones determining** who was "saved or damned," as part of this philosophy/worldview.

These early Calvinist-oriented settlers in the 1600's were primarily Puritans, and they did not believe in a central religious authority such as a Pope, bishop, or any such religious person. These early settlers also weren't interested in converting the Indians as the Spanish priests had pursued in Mexico. This was a critical difference between the Europeans. The Spaniards answered to a higher central figure, who wanted Indian converts to combat the recent threat of Protestantism, and thus, the Pope enlisted his priests as protectors of the Indians in order to convert them, especially after the appearance of Tonantzin, aka *la Virgen de Guadalupe*, in 1531. The Calvinist-oriented Protestants answered to no such "higher authority," and they individually were not inclined to convert the Indians. Their purpose was to pursue individual wealth and expand their settlements while practicing their radical Protestantism.

The only central authority these extremist Protestants answered to was the Bible. The Bible, of course, is a compilation of books/texts written over a span between 300-1500 years. It can literally be interpreted in so many ways that justification can be found for anything. The Calvinist approach to Christianity was to use the Bible to justify all their colonial actions, especially actions taken against the Indians. The Calvinist Protestants made no apologies and offered little justification for anything they did in swallowing the lands of the Indians. In their view and interpretation of the Bible, God had pre-determined that the white man was "saved," and therefore entitled to all the material gains they could achieve by any means necessary; while the Indians were "damned," and therefore deserved the "fate," that they received at the hands of the "saved" white man.

Thus, U.S. history records no justification or apology for literally stealing all of the original thirteen colonies and eventually all the lands east of the Mississippi from our Native American relatives. U.S. history also doesn't discuss the murder of the Native American to achieve the theft of these lands. U.S. history just wants you to assume, **_abracadabra, that after the feast of the first Thanksgiving_**, miraculously the white man assumed control of all the lands east of the Mississippi, and the Indian was compliant or silent during this entire period.

The same Calvinist philosophy/approach applied to slavery. Again, for the Calvinists, God had "damned" the Black race, so there was no need to apologize for enslaving them and their descendants. The existence of slaves, torture, rape, abuse, breaking up of slave families; any justification needed, could be found in the Bible. Likewise, U.S. history doesn't apologize or bother to justify initiating a war in 1845 against a newly born Mexico, in order to steal Texas and all the lands west of the Mississippi, under the made-up "Doctrine of Manifest Destiny." What is "manifest destiny," if not an assertion that God has so sanctioned?

Here again, the white man was the "saved one," and therefore entitled to subjugate and steal from the "damned" Mexicans (of course, the truth is that all lands taken were Native American, which lands Mexico had no legitimate title to, since title derived from the illegal Spanish colonizer). The Native American also wasn't consulted when France "sold" their lands to white America under the "Louisiana Purchase." This Calvinist worldview of no apologies, and justifying all political, military, societal and economic actions taken during the creation of the United States, has been the foundation of white supremacy and privilege in this country since its birth.

But these examples are but the better-known theft of lands the gringo has shoved under the rug or justified. Lands beyond "Manifest

Destiny" were added after the Spanish-American War in 1898. The populations of Puerto Rico, Cuba, the Philippines, Guam, and the Marianas, had no say or representation as they became colonial subjects of the United States. But perhaps the worst theft was the overthrown of the Kingdom of Hawaii. When the first Christian missionaries arrived in Hawaii in 1820, the lands of every island were the undivided property of the island king. The missionaries quickly discovered they could gain power by marrying the various royal princesses on each island. After marrying the royal princesses, the missionaries established the registered division of lands by surveyors so they could claim legal title to the lands based on their marriage to the princesses.

Not satisfied with the acquisition of most of the islands by subterfuge, the descendants of the missionaries and their fellow white Americans demanded the resignation of Hawaii's Queen in 1893, at the risk of having her palace bombarded by an American warship in the harbor. This was the unlawful overthrow of a recognized international country, the Kingdom of Hawaii, both by subterfuge as well as military force. Once again, this episode is a part of US history that is either ignored or glazed over with minimal commentary, as hula dancers sway in the trade winds.

In 2021, we are seeing this Calvinist history of white supremacy and privilege through their "saved and damned" philosophy, being challenged by the subject of critical race theory. The introduction of the importance of race in the unfolding of history is being opposed and outlawed where they can by the Republicans and modern-day Calvinists. **What do they fear if critical race theory is mandated in school curriculums?** An honest discussion on the role of race in the history of the United States, which, for white supremacists, is against their interests.

Fortunately, Life always seeks a balance to everything, regardless of human politics. Balance and harmony are the natural order of the Universe, of the Great Spirit. The Puritan extremist worldview of believing that they could determine who God had "saved or damned," was tempered by its Duality, which also emerged from the Puritans: **Democracy.** Democracy in the 1600's was just an idea floating around Europe, and being promoted in England by John Locke, who had Calvinist leanings. Because the extremist Protestants fleeing England were being persecuted by an autocratic King, they opposed the King's manner of governance by applying democratic organization to their congregations, when they came in the 1600's.

The Calvinists used democracy amongst themselves to further distinguish themselves from the autocratic England ruled by a King. The use of democracy by the Puritans in organizing their congregations then spread to their politics, which in turn created the thirteen colonies. By the time the Founding Fathers met to draft the Constitution in 1787 after the Revolutionary War, the dual side of the Calvinists in promoting democracy was the politics of the day. Two years later, in 1789, the French Revolution spread the winds of democracy across Europe as well.

It was the Calvinist belief in democracy which fueled and authored the Constitution the "Founding Fathers" created, with its idealistic visions for a democratic society. However, this Calvinist democracy only applied to the white man, not to the Native American or the Black slave. After all, the Founding Fathers were Calvinists, which meant they still also believed in the "saved and damned" approach. Yet, decades later in 1830, a growing belief in democracy within Calvinism started questioning the morality of slavery. When these democratic values grew more widespread, they were challenged by the proponents of slavery in 1861.

Native Americans never had any strong advocates during the history of this country to cause a civil war questioning the actions taken against them. They were always viewed as expendable and an obstacle to possessing all the lands without challenge to its use. The genocide against Native Americans and the theft of their lands is the *Original Sin* of the United States. The *Second Sin was slavery*. This fact continues to be overlooked today, when reparations are discussed for Blacks while the Original Sin against the Native American is conveniently ignored, much less discussed. Also forgotten is that "Buffalo Soldier Blacks" killed Native Americans as well.

The Civil War philosophically was between the "saved and

damned," and the "democracy," wings of Calvinism. Even though the "democracy" wing won over the "saved/damned" wing, the "saved/damned" proponents continued to use white supremacy and privilege to dilute or deny democratic access to Blacks and nonwhites. For the next hundred years, the white supremacy and privilege agenda continued under both the Democrats as well as the Republicans. After the Civil Rights Bill of 1964, the Republican party has evolved into the standard bearer for white supremacy and privilege. To counter them, Democrats have morphed into the defenders of Democracy.

The continuing evolution of democracy introduced the Civil Rights Act of 1964 to push back against the white supremacy racist wings of both political parties. World War II had demonstrated the strength and value Mexicans, Blacks, Asians, and other minorities who fought in US uniforms had contributed. All these events produced sizable gains by all minority communities in the 1960-70's, powered by monies from the War on Poverty. The 1980's saw white supremacy push-back ushered in by Reagan. This white supremacy push-back has continued since, with the erosion of Affirmative Action and Ethnic Studies in higher education, and recent Supreme Court assaults on the 1964 Voting Rights Bill.

The Republican party started out as the main opponent to the "saved or damned" Calvinists who practiced slavery. The Republicans were the party of Lincoln, and thus, opponents to the "saved/damned" slavers. But even in the 1860's, the GOP remained true to a belief in white supremacy, in the same way the "Founding Fathers" had been. Both the Constitution and the Emancipation Proclamation had fine print attached, meaning their idealistic concepts had limited intended application.

After the Civil Rights Bill of 1964 passed, the southern Democrats became Republicans overnight. The Republicans, who had supported Johnson to pass the Bill, saw an opportunity to re-gain power by accepting the defecting southern Democrats. The Republicans have walked a tightrope since, pursuing the promotion of white supremacy and privilege while representing the wealthy, and forming a partnership with the "saved/damned" Calvinists. They accomplished this partnership by courting the leaders of the evangelical community and supporting the evangelical "right to life" agenda.

We might be seeing the beginnings of a new type of Civil War in this country. The duality of the Calvinists is at war with itself once again, in what is being described as "culture wars." "Culture wars" is more politically correct than simply saying what it means: ***"the non-whites are coming after what's ours!"*** The white supremacists see their privileged status being threatened by a coalition of growing minorities and democratic-oriented white Americans. The white supremacists know that the demographics of this country will turn minority dominant by 2045.

Just as the South sought to extend and maintain a form of slavery by enacting restrictive laws against Blacks, the white supremacists are using modern-day tactics of appointing conservative federal judges, controlling state legislatures, and enacting restrictive legislation aimed at limiting the right to vote. Passing laws making it a crime to give food/water to anyone waiting in line to vote. Passing laws where politicians can overrule the vote count and declare their own victors.

The Republican white supremacists have the support of the "saved/damned" descendants of the Puritans, the evangelical community. The evangelicals continue to justify support for a right-wing agenda because they jointly are anti-abortion. Evangelicals are the largest religious community in the country, with about 85 million members, a quarter of the population. About 75% of evangelicals are white. Approximately 80% of all evangelicals vote Republican, regardless of the color of skin.

These are the "bedrock" voters of the Republican party in this country, and they ironically support the white wealthy class even though many are in the lower economic classes. In the evangelical mind, supporting a white right-wing agenda benefitting the wealthy is okay, if fetuses get to live. These politics are a modern version of using Biblical interpretations to sustain the political beliefs of their reverends, in this case, being anti-abortion and promoting "right to life."

On the other side, the democratic Calvinists have thankfully become more numerous than at any time in our history as a country.

The white female has become the most common democrat, especially the suburban mother, and she is starting to influence her children to become more tolerant as well. This use of female energy by the Great Spirit, to balance the extremist white supremacy male-dominated side of Calvinism, should not be underestimated.

It is the natural order of Life, our native ancestors learned, to seek balance and harmony amongst diversity. In thankful unity with the white democratic Calvinists are most of the members of the minority communities of this country. Together, this coalition between the white democratic Calvinists and minorities, is what is promoting the positive evolution of democracy in this country.

Yet, the anti-Christ aka 45 and the Republicans were able to make substantial gains amongst sectors of different minority communities in the elections of 2020. Gains made despite the social repression and racism the anti-Christ aka 45 openly promoted during the four years of his presidency. In Florida, the GOP gained amongst the Cubans and other white refugees from Colombia, Venezuela, and Latin America. These communities are generally white and fled their home countries because they lost some or all of their prior white privileges. They support white supremacy and privilege in this country because they benefit from it.

The *tejanos* and other minorities who voted for the GOP? Certainly, these are examples of how deep and pervasive the colonial mentality has become accepted by these minority voters. It is no coincidence that Mexicans in Texas identify with being *tejano*, rather than Mexican. *Tejanos* are unique in the sense they have developed their own music, food, and culture. Ironically, this has contributed to a belief amongst many *tejanos*, that they are not the same as the Mexicans just across the Rio Grande. With at least 40% of Texas' population, one would think Raza would have significant political power in the state. The truth is otherwise, confirming the colonized state of mind many *tejanos* continue to suffer from.

In 2021, a significant rise in consciousness amongst the democratic Calvinists is their awareness of recent police killings and brutality. George Floyd's death captured on video seems to have finally been the "straw that broke the camel's back," in that the democratic wing is now actively questioning the existence of police brutality and white supremacy in this country. The issues of excessive police force and the white supremacist assault on the Capitol Building on January 6, have finally placed the reality of white supremacy and racism squarely on the center of the national table. This awareness and rise in consciousness by the democratic wing further blunt the ability of the Republican white supremacists to continue their privileged agenda.

These examples and recent events clarify that the most important First Step of decolonization is to be secure about your identity while you elevate your culture. For those Chicanos who have known no other identity other than Chicano, this important first step is already a given. Identity can start to blur, however, once that young Chicanita/o enters high school and certainly college. Suddenly, students are in multi-cultural environments, and become aware of the multiple identities a Chicano can wear on any given day. *Hispanic, Latino, Latinx, Chicanx;* which set of clothes do you like? Which identity works better for you on this day or occasion? Raza students hear our politicos, academicians, and business leaders identify as Latino or Hispanic. *Seldom to never do they hear Mexican or Chicano*.

"What's the big deal, don't get hung-up on labels. Let the young generation have their say," some declare.   My response is, *if you want to de-colonize, is there a bigger deal than your identity?*

In his classic book, *"The Colonizer and the Colonized"* (1965), Albert Memmi outlined the methodologies employed by the colonizer in order to subdue and control the colonized.   Central to the strategy used by all colonizers is to minimize, or better yet, destroy the institutions, religion, culture, and identity of the colonized persons. In other words, make the colonized so meek and insecure that he offers no threat to your dominance. The Spanish executed this policy towards our native ancestors after 1519.

In the United States, the gabacho has pursued the same strategy towards most, if not all, minorities. Mexicans/Chicanos had no effective self-governance until the 1970's, despite some towns/ cities having huge percentages of Raza comprising their populations for decades. The Catholic priests eagerly tended to the immigrating Mexicans, who quickly became the majority of the congregations. Those Mexicans who had been practicing syncretic Catholicism in Mexico now encountered the very conservative Roman Catholicism, which considers the Vatican to be liberal. An elementary school education was what most Mexicans hoped to achieve in this country until the 1950's. As long as the Mexican stayed quiet and worked the fields, he was allowed to eat his beans. Periodically, however, his community would get "harvested," like the mass deportations of the 1930's.

With the rise of the political Chicano identity in the late 1960's, white supremacy advocates of both parties became alarmed. Being "Chicano" signaled a defiant, anti-assimilationist identity, that questioned the values and path to the "American dream." It also powered huge gains for Mexicans in many different sectors within the United States society, because of the numbers of Raza students graduating from colleges. This combination of a defiant identity that reached for goals other than the "American dream," threatened the interests of the white supremacist.

In 1977, the government's OMB office collaborated with Mexican Americans to introduce "Hispanic" as a new identity. The purpose of this collaboration was to counter the growing acceptance of "Chicano" by the Mexican community. The government bureaucrats and their Mexican American friends wanted to counter with an identity meant to promote integration and assimilation into the gabacho's society. ***"Something more European, more gentrified, more "inclusive."*** They thus invented and applied "Hispanic," to all Spanish-surnamed persons in the government surveys.

This assault on our identity continued in the early 1990's. Because "Hispanic" was being resisted by many Raza, the media (Los Angeles Times) introduced "Latino" as a new umbrella. For Chicanos, Latino was historically identifiable as a person from Latin America, not from Mexico. But a Mexican American columnist at the Times, opposed to "Chicano," persisted in promoting "Latino" in column after column.

Eventually, Latino was included in the 2000 census as an identity choice, along with Hispanic.

"Mexican/Chicano" were NOT included as identities until the 2020 US census, but ONLY after you identified first as "Latino," and then checked a sub-category of being "Mexican/Chicano." To the gringo and his compliant Mexican Americans, the fact that Mexicans have been in the United States for centuries, constitute two-thirds (2/3) of all Spanish-surnamed persons in the country, and are descended from our neighboring country, is irrelevant. The identity of being Mexican remains silent/ignored on US news and media.

The assault on our true identity of being Mexican/Chicano are daily reinforced by the media and others, who refer to Mexicans/Chicanos as Latinos in their public declarations. Some Chicanos rationalize using Latino because it is more "inclusive" of non-Mexicans. Since when is "Latino" inclusive of Mexicans? Why can't they say "Mexican/Chicano and Latinos?" Wouldn't this clarification be more truthful and inclusive at the same time?

This deliberate consistent assault to confuse the Chicano about his identity, is the hand of the colonizer at work, against the colonized (Mexicans/Chicanos). In the early 2000's, Latinx appeared as an identity to distinguish those Latinos who did not identify with either the male or female sex. More recently, Chicanx has appeared with the same purpose, yet Chicanx can be the identity of "sensitive males/females," as well as non-binary Chicanos.

When viewed from a native historical perspective, Chicanx is consistent with pueblos having different names for their non-binary members. In the Native American pueblos, "two spirit, winkte," and many other names, were associated with tribal LGBTQ+ members. The same occurred amongst the more-closeted Mexican pueblos, with "muxe (Zapotec) and nawiki" (Raramuri), being two known names for these folks. So Chicanx is only different from that tradition in that some straight males and females are also choosing to identify with their non-binary *carnalas y carnales y otros.*

Returning to the issue of identity, and its importance, let's consider how the identity a Mexican chooses in the United States indicates the colonial status of her/his consciousness. Obviously, we will be making general conclusions for which exceptions can certainly be found. To re-state the obvious, to be colonized is to accept the worldview of the colonizer as superior to yours. For a Mexican in the United States, being colonized means to accept that the American worldview which includes white supremacy and privilege, is superior to your own culture and worldview. A colonized person expresses this support of white America's worldview, by choosing an identity they think will give them greater mobility/accommodation, within the gabacho society.

A colonized Raza thus chooses identities like Latin-American, Spanish-American, Hispanic, Latino, Latinx, Mexican American, and American of Mexican descent. These identities all have one thing in common. These are all acceptable identities to the gabacho, because they all pursue assimilation into his society and don't challenge his white privilege. Even though we all know that white America would really prefer you to be anything but Mexican, which means Latino is preferable to Mexican American, and American of Mexican descent is better, for the gabacho, if it loses the last three words.

Thus, the first obvious step for you to de-colonize yourself, is to choose an identity of your own choosing, rather than one meant to please the gabacho. It doesn't have to be Chicano; Mexican (even tejano) will do just fine. Though in reality, "Chicano" is just a US version of a Mexican, since it linguistically evolved from mexicano (mechicano), and before that, Mexica (meshica). The key here is your conciencia; that is what really matters in whatever identity you select. The consciousness necessary here, is one of "me/we."

We have been discussing those Raza who are still battling with the issue of their identity, meaning they sometimes identify as something other than Chicano. Let's move on to those of us who have been Chicano since birth, or at least for many years now.

Think of the "Chicano" as being the *"profundos"* of the Mexican community of the United States. The Chicano is the common woman and man: farmworkers, janitors, maids, restaurant workers, bus drivers, housewives, *chavalitos y chavalitas, viejitos y viejitas*, of the barrios. But we are also elementary, high school, and college students; along with being some of their teachers/professors. Some of us do *danza azteca* and are re-connecting with our native side in multiple ways. Some Chicana/os are cooking dishes with their mothers and abuelas, keeping dishes alive for future generations and bettering them at the same time.

What is being discussed is our culture and its importance to our general/mental wellbeing. Our culture is both essentially native in foundation/worldview, and cosmic, albeit unconsciously, in projection. The Red Nations culture of the original pueblos of Mexico, which culture the mestizo shares, provided our ancestors with the will and guidance to continue to live meaningful human and cosmic lives. It should be learned, nourished, and promoted as part of your decolonization. It is the well of strength that will always be there for you to draw from and will provide the clarity to navigate you through the gringo's fog.

Now that we have revealed the gabacho's true history in creating the United States, the Second Step of your de-colonization should be deconstructing the gringo's white supremacy and privileged beliefs. The need for this deconstruction is logical, given the true history of the United States, including the fact that ALL the lands were taken through murder/military force/theft from the Native Americans. Morally, there is not enough forgiveness in any religion to justify what the European did in stealing these lands. Making matters even more extreme, the Calvinists sought to obliterate the various cultures of the Native American pueblos by placing them into prisons, aka reservations.

The deconstruction of the gringo's true history reveals the source of his *spiritual poverty*. His actions in creating this country are returning to him, per the Law of Causation, and the return of this historical negative energy is the spiritual poverty which manifests itself daily in many different forms. The cult worship of the Big Lie and the anti-Christ aka 45, the cheating/fixing of elections, the packing of conservative ideologues in the courts, the sowing of distrust in the nation's institutions and norms, the willingness to subvert democracy to retain power.

Yet, despite his spiritual poverty and historical illegality as a foreign occupier of these lands, the modern-day Calvinist, Democrat or Republican, still believes that he can decide who is entitled to live on these native lands. The white supremacist within him arrogantly declares that certain members of native pueblos, those coming from Mexico and the triangle Central American countries, are "illegal aliens." We know that the true illegal alien is in fact the European and his descendants, who as the ruling colonizers have created a false history of nation-building and "values," with the intent to maintain their grip on power. Deconstruction also demands rejection for any justification the white man may propose, for bringing kidnapped Africans against their will, to become slave labor for 300 years, so the white man could enjoy his society of white supremacy and privilege.

Our decolonization thus demands a rejection of MOST of the gabacho's values, for they were formed on a foundation of murder, theft, and slavery. Formed on a foundation that he could determine who was "saved/damned," and use this Big Lie to justify his anti-humanity actions against those who were non-European. Because the gringo's worldview is based on a false belief in his white supremacy and privilege, it should also place in doubt what he promotes as his GOALS.

"Is the obsession with securing more and more material wealth what Chicanos also want? Is the gringo's belief valid, that whatever negative consequences his quest for material gain produces, is just incidental collateral damage? Collateral damage that can be ignored or "forgiven" through a dunk in water, or at the confessional? Do Chicanos want to adopt the gringo's preference for individual gain, even if such gain is at the expense of our community? Is the gringo's rejection of Mother Earth as a living being, and therefore pursuing naked exploitation of her natural resources, for the greater good of Chicanos? Do Chicanos need to purchase insurance to live a lifetime? Should Chicanos accept economic dominance by a small group of the extreme-wealthy? Should Chicanos be willing to continue to send our children to fight foreign wars?"

What about *"lifting yourself by your bootstraps,"* and the *"American dream;"* do they exist? Yes, they are possible, and we have seen numerous examples of minority individuals who have attained and continue to attain high positions within our society. Minority individuals, not minority communities. I came from a farmworker background and became a college professor and lawyer before moving to Hawaii in 1990. There, after lawyering for a couple of years, I became a tortillero. Yes, a *tortillero* who makes tortillas for a living. A *tortillero* more economically successful than being a lawyer. Retired now.

So yes, many things are possible in this society. The key to assimilating material success is your consciousness. One of my abuelo's mantras was **"el hombre no se vende"** (you are not for sale). I have kept that mantra steady throughout the successes in my life that I have experienced. Numerous opportunities presented themselves throughout my life for greater material comforts, but at the cost of compromising myself. Not for sale.

Thus, achieve all you are able to, so long as you don't sell yourself to gain the achievements. Reject the European vision of the "me/my ego," and instead steer your life ship to the native "me/we." The native individual vision of "me/we," is that of *conciencia* (consciousness); that is the *conciencia* of the Chicano that distinguishes him from the Mexican American and other assimilationist identities.

While most of the gringo's values deserve rejection; DEMOCRACY, however, is a value which merits our support. We do, after all, live in this wonderful multiracial experiment called the United States. For all its imperfections and flaws, it remains one of the best places to live in the world. For Chicanos, supporting democracy is a win-win. It is a win-win because democracy advances the Chicano/Mexican agenda in many ways positive to our communities. It is also a win-win because democracy allows the freedom for decolonized Chicanos to function progressively and actively within the society yet pursue a transformation onto your Chicano Red Road. Democracy does not demand that you remain a Christian in order to support it; to the contrary, democracy promotes the diversity to include all faiths under its umbrella.

After deconstruction of the gringo legacy, we must remain clear-eyed about the democracy we support. The democracy Chicanos should support is the idealism of people actually deciding in fair elections who should represent them and how things should run for the benefit of all. Our current version of "democracy," that has billionaires and corporations controlling the economics and politics of this country, is NOT the democracy we should support. It is NOT the democracy we should support, because the concentration of wealth and power in individuals and corporations, is NOT democracy; it is elitism and authoritarian for the benefit of the wealthy and privileged few.

After securing our identity as Chicanos and deconstructing while reviewing the gabacho's true history of the United States, we must reject most of his values while retaining support for Democracy. How can we support values which are based on lies, deceit, murder, and slavery? At the end of the day, democracy remains a work in progress around the world, more advanced in some countries than others. It is still arguably the best system to administer a country, especially a country such as the United States, with the most diverse society on Earth.

That leaves the 800-pound gorilla that needs to be examined. The 800-pound gorilla is Christianity. Remember, the process of decolonization calls for you to deconstruct the colonial ideologies of the colonizer. Christianity has ALWAYS been the colonial ideology of the colonizer, whether the colonizer be the Spaniard or the gringo. If Chicanos want to decolonize from the European legacy, it is critical that you recognize and understand the European's religion/worldview and its role in promoting white supremacy and privilege.

The European developed the religion from Middle East roots, interpreted it to justify his white superiority, and has nourished and promoted it for the last two thousand years. In return, the Christian religion, through its mutations from Catholicism to Protestantism, has faithfully continued to promote the privilege and superiority of the European. It has done so in the practice of the religion in many subtle and overt ways.

It is time to brew some more Chinese mud for this analysis of Christianity. All Catholic popes throughout its 2,000+ year history have been White. All the Protestant leaders (Luther, Calvin, Roberts, Graham, etc.) were/are White. The Mormons were founded by a White American who based their religion on White supremacy. Over 95% of all Catholic saints are White. Jesus was White. The Virgin Mary and Joseph were White. Michelangelo painted God as a White man on the Vatican ceiling. Throughout this analysis, the Chinese mud has remained almost WHITE, while thickening; confirming that Christianity is the religion that nourishes and sustains the European's white supremacy and privilege. The dark sugar of Martin Luther King, Jr., is the *"almost"* on the White.

Some Christian churches may say that the white supremacy perspective is in the past, that modern Christianity is more inclusive and tolerant of minorities. Really? Believing that the Christian churches are more inclusive of minorities is like accepting that the "American dream" is real for everyone, and that you can actually "lift yourself up by your bootstraps." If any aspects of Christianity are now more "inclusive," it is because they are competing for dwindling church attendees. Competing for new members, while continuing to promote white supremacy and privilege in matters that count.

Christianity is what it has always been: the worldview/religion of the white man/European/colonizer. The evangelical still promotes that he is "saved" because he is "pro-life;" while those supporting abortion are "damned." Any modifications this colonizer worldview has done to include more minorities, are exactly that: modifications, not a total change, of its historical white supremacy and privilege message. Modifications intended to give you, as the colonized, the illusion that you have a place at the table; when in fact, you are eating in the basement with the servants, while the white Europeans gorge themselves upstairs at the table of plenty.

Part Four
Aztlan

…we declare the independence of our Mestizo nation, a Bronze people with a Bronze culture

…Alurista

1

The spiritual Aztlan

Part of the culture of most, if not all, societies/civilizations, is the concept of an afterlife. Humans want to believe there is some type of existence after our life ends. Believing in an afterlife can introduce an extraordinary energy into your life, giving direction and purpose. For many people the world over, faith and belief in an afterlife is what gives them a reason for living, especially those persons living in extreme poverty or in a violent society. While the belief in an afterlife may be totally based on faith for many persons, for many of the indigenous communities of the world, interaction with the spirit world is common enough to conclude that an afterlife exists. It is only the "developed and civilized" societies of the world, which question whether an afterlife/spirit world exists.

The Vikings had their Valhalla; the Chinese, Diyu; the Hindus, the seven Lokas; the Buddhists, Nirvana; the Christians, Heaven or Hell; the Muslims, Akhirah; and the Mayans/Toltecs/Aztecs, **Tamoanchan**. Thus, for our purposes, the potential afterlife of interest is **Tamoanchan**, for the Christian heaven and hell has already been extensively considered and hoped for/feared, in our history as colonial subjects to both the Spaniards and the white Americans.

Considering that Life is as the Mexica believed, cyclical; the Law of Causation mandates that this afterlife be where our spirits originated from, before providing the consciousness for the material bodies from Mother Earth. After all, the transition from spirit to matter is a movement of energy. Thus, where is **Tamoanchan**, the afterlife the Mayans, Toltecs, and Aztecs, sought? Could it be the same place as Aztlan?

"Aztlan" is one of those historical names with an uncertain past. An uncertain past like Stonehenge.   The rock sculpture in England is there, but we don't know for sure who built it. The Serpent Mounds in Ohio are visible, but their uncertain past is that no one knows for sure who created this longest serpentine structure in the world. There are multiple examples throughout history of similar locations who have uncertain origins.

In the case of Aztlan, we know it existed because the people who originated from there, the Aztecs, declared such as part of their oral history. But the story of their journey from Aztlan, which some believe began approximately in the year 1000, was already a distant memory when the surviving Aztecs/Mexicas related this history 500 years later to the gachupine.

The Aztecs/Mexicas collaborating with the Spanish writers could only recount that Aztlan was "in the northern lands of the heron." Unfortunately for our purposes, the heron is widespread throughout North America, so that doesn't help much in focusing on a location. "Northern" could mean any lands north of Tenochtitlan, which would include central and northern Mexico, as well as the entire western United States, all the way north to southern Canada (all areas populated by herons). Thus, arriving at any certainty as to Aztlan's physical location based on "northern lands of herons," is like throwing darts. Anywhere on that board might qualify.

So, let's be honest. Chicanos might romantically insist that Aztlan was in the US Southwest, but the evidence shows there is no basis to insist with certainty on that location, given the definition of "northern lands" above. Furthermore, why alienate some relatives, like the Navajo, Apache, Pueblo and others; who would be threatened if Chicanos insisted on the speculation that Aztlan was in the Southwest, meaning somewhere in the lands these relatives occupy? *No vale la pena.* Part of traveling on the Red Road, as has been shown, is maintaining the cosmic harmony. Furthermore, how can we start traveling towards a physical Aztlan, if we don't know for sure where our destination is located?

A stark example of an unsure location is the speculation that the pronunciation, and spelling, of "Aztlan," was the result of the new addition to the Spanish language, the lisp. The Spaniards added the *lisp* to their oral language in the 1500's, and the conjecture here is that the Aztecs actually told the Spaniards that they had come from ATLAN. However, the Spanish applied the lisp to Atlan, and voila, Athlan came out, eventually pronounced and spelled as Aztlan!

Adding to this speculation is that ATLAN was the Nahuatl name the maestro Andres gave to Atlantis, which he claimed the Aztec Nation had originated from before it sank. He wrote the Mexica Prayer at the start of this book in the 1970's. In it, he clearly mentions **"the Spirit Guides of the Atlante-Tolteca tradition."**

In *"Mitakuye Oyasin: We are all related,"* (1989), the Dakota author spends an entire chapter reciting the possible Atlantis roots of numerous original pueblos of Native Americans. But Atlantis remains speculative as a possible physical Aztlan.

Thus, the Aztlan we wish to travel to on the Red Road is the *spiritual Aztlan*, the homeland of the Chicano. Where is this *spiritual Aztlan* and how did it become the homeland of the Chicano? The *spiritual Aztlan* was born in 1969 with a poetic declaration that it existed; and which also defined it as the homeland of the Chicano. Just as the Declaration of Independence created the United States, and the *Grito de Dolores* announced the birth of Mexico, the poet Alurista declared the existence of Aztlan, the Chicano homeland. This declaration occurred at the National Youth Liberation Conference hosted by Corky Gonzales at Denver, Colorado, in late March, 1969.

When we walk on the Red Road, we recognize that the occurrence of events happens because they are mandated/allowed by the Great Spirit. That is another example of the Law of Compensation at work, the unfolding of history being dictated by the Will of God, *la Voluntad de Dios*. Ultimately, all events in Life occur because, as the maestro would declare, *"estaban programados"* (they were destined).

Thus, the *spiritual Aztlan* was molded and created by the spirit world and the Cosmic Consciousness, which then expressed themselves through the poet, Alurista. The fact that it happened, confirms that it was ***programado***; it was destined by the Will of God. Before thousands of Raza youths from throughout the country in attendance, Alurista shouted out his spiritually mandated declaration:

"Preamble to the Plan Espiritual de Aztlan"

"In the spirit of a new people that is conscious not only of its proud historical heritage, but also of the brutal "Gringo" invasion of our territories, we, the Chicano inhabitants and civilizers of the Northern land of Aztlán, from whence came our forefathers, reclaiming the land of their birth and consecrating the determination of our people of the Sun, declare that the call of our blood is our power, our response and our inevitable destiny.

We are free and sovereign to determine those tasks which are justly called for by our house, the sweat of our brows and by our hearts. Aztlán belongs to those that plant the seeds, water the land and gather the crops, and not to foreign Europeans. We do not recognize capricious frontiers on the Bronze Continent.

Brotherhood unites us, and love of our brothers makes us a people whose time has come and who struggle against the foreign "Gabacho" who exploits our riches and destroys our culture. With our hearts in our hands and our hands in the soil, we declare the independence of our Mestizo nation, a Bronze people with a Bronze culture. Before the world, before all of North America, before our brothers in the Bronze continent, we are a Nation of free pueblos, we are Aztlán."

Let us consider this spiritually energized declaration paragraph by paragraph. In the first paragraph, Chicanos are defined as conscious "new people" whose "call of our blood" is both our power as well as our destiny. Chicanos are also said to inhabit the northern land of Aztlan, the land of our Aztec forefathers. Though this wording does infer a physical Aztlan, it is a conclusion based on speculation rather than fact. It can thus be interpreted to refer to either a physical or a *spiritual Aztlan*.

From a physical perspective, it conveniently places Aztlan in the United States since this is where Chicanos live. But where exactly in the United States? When the declaration was made, Chicanos lived primarily in the Southwest. But even in 1969 Chicanos had been in Chicago, Michigan, and other northern locales for decades. Does a "northern location" of Aztlan have to refer to the geography of the Earth? Could it not be referring to the northern sky above us, alluding to a cosmic Aztlan?

Continuing, a "conscious new people" here refers to mestizos, the blend of Red/White that emerged from *la Conquista*. But these are not just any mestizo; rather, these are mestizos who have become conscious (Chicanos) of who they are and value their indigenous ancestry. What is more interesting is the "call of our blood," which turns out to be "our power and destiny."

This "call of our blood" is a declaration that we are free human beings within the Red Nations with our own cosmic destiny. We create this destiny individually and jointly through our actions which is our power as human beings interacting with the Universe. The call of our blood thus is the existing power and purpose of the Red Nations within the experience we call Life.

The second paragraph continues with the theme of freedom and self-determination. Aztlan is declared free from European ownership beliefs because Aztlan is part of Mother Earth. Our Mother Earth who nourishes us cannot be owned by any human being. She is a living being with her own soul and spirit. The paragraph ends with a visualization that at some point in the future, the borders that the Europeans have established on the Turtle continents shall turn to dust.

The third paragraph is arguably the strongest, and with the most impactful messages. It starts with a declaration that Chicanos are part of a Raza brotherhood that is aware of its colonized status. The next sentence is perhaps the most significant in the entire *"Preamble..."* Alurista declares the **emergence of a Mestizo Nation composed of bronze people with a Bronze culture.** Both the emergence of a Mestizo Nation as well as the color identification of Bronze are very significant here.

Why Bronze rather than brown? Brown is a color onto itself; Hindus and Arabs are brown. Whereas Bronze is a **brownish shade of Red**. Bronze is the color on the cover of this book. Because Bronze is a shade of Red, Alurista's spiritual intention is clear: the Mestizo Nation of Aztlan is part of the Red Nations!

Let's get philosophical to consider the *spiritual Aztlan*. The Mexica worldview the maestro Andres described was cyclical, as are the Hindu and Buddhist worldviews. Believing that Life is cyclical means you believe in reincarnation. In turn, this means a belief in the continuation of consciousness, as it evolves into the next life. Cyclical also means that all energy that moves (the Cause) must return to where it began.

Thus, if Aztlan is the homeland from which our forefathers came (the Cause), then this cyclical worldview means the Chicana/o must return to this homeland, which will be a *spiritual Aztlan*, upon her/his "death." This cycle would comply with the Law of Causation. This is also the afterlife envisioned by our ancestors; a return to our spiritual homeland in order to prepare for the next material lifetime. So, where in the cosmos, might this *spiritual Aztlan* exist?

Earlier, the question was posed as to the possible existence of a cosmic Aztlan beyond the northern sky. Early in my relationship with the maestro Andres, the subject about the Bering Strait theory being the origins of the Red Nations people came up. The maestro quickly dismissed the Bering Strait theory, declaring instead that **"venimos de** (we came from) **Andromeda."** By stating that the Mexica (and other original pueblos) came from Andromeda, he was saying that their spirits had journeyed from Andromeda to give life/consciousness to the human bodies Mother Earth was providing. Following the cyclical Law of Causation, he was thus inferring that upon death, our spirits return to our ancestral spiritual homeland, located in the Andromeda galaxy.

I considered his comment on Andromeda being the origin of the Red Nations spirits as interesting/speculative and then forgot about it. How could anyone prove it, or not? Years later, reading Archie Fire Lame Deer, the Lakota medicine man, commenting where Lakota spirits go to after death, he said: *"According to Lakota belief, when a person dies, his or her nagi, or spirit, starts its journey to the spirit land, the Land of Many Lodges. It walks along the Wanagi Tachanku, the spirit trail, which whites call the Milky Way."* (Gift of Power: *The Life and Teachings of a Lakota Medicine Man"*, p.146).

In the infinite vastness of the Universe, the galaxy closest to our own Milky Way galaxy is Andromeda. Andromeda is literally our next-door spacial neighbor. While Lame Deer didn't specify Andromeda as the destination of the Lakota spirit, if the Lakota spirit walks along the Milky Way spirit trail on its way to the spirit land, doesn't it make sense that the Land of Many Lodges, the spirit land, is just beyond the Milky Way, in Andromeda? This statement by Lame Deer suddenly gave validity to the maestro's Andromeda origins statement, and why I believe the *spiritual Aztlan* is located in Andromeda.

We started this discussion by mentioning the hoped-for destination of the Mayan/Toltec/Aztec spirit, **Tamoanchan**. What connection could there be between **Tamoanchan** and the *spiritual Aztlan*? **Tamoanchan**, its meaning and its location, has largely remained a mystery since la Conquista. The Spanish writers never understood the paradise **Tamoanchan** represented, which is why one description is that of a "mythical place where humans were made from blood and the bones of Mictlan (death)." Another description is that **Tamoanchan** is where the Aztec, Toltec, and Mayan spirits would go to after death; but first, they had to face and overcome the challenges of Xibalba (underworld), before the spirit could get to **Tamoanchan**. In their own way, both descriptions are somewhat correct.

Let's do a quick Panche Be analysis on **Tamoanchan**. Consistent with the Law of Causation, all energy returns to where it began. The analysis continues, understanding that our ancestors used metaphors to teach the lessons of their stories. Thus, the *Tamoanchan* where humans are made from "blood and bones," refers to the spirit world and the process of the transition from spirit to matter. As part of this transition, the spirit must first enter Xibalba, the Nine Underworlds, where the lower stages of spiritual evolution occur. *Tamoanchan* is thus the 13 Heavens, where spirits undergo their final evolutions before being re-born as a human. Since the final transformations from spirit to matter occurs in *Tamoanchan*, to *Tamoanchan* it must return, according to the Law of Causation.

The meaning of *Tamoanchan* by the Mayan maestro and linguist, Domingo Martinez Paredez, revealed its location. In the Yucatec Mayan language, *Tamoanchan* is translated as: TA, or "place," MOAN, "bird." and CHAN, "Serpent." This translates literally as the "Place of the Bird and the Serpent." Metaphorically, the "Place of the Bird and Serpent," is another way of saying "the Home of the Feathered Serpent."

Once again, the Feathered Serpent is the representative of the Great Spirit. Thus, the "Home of the Feathered Serpent" metaphorically means "where the Great Spirit resides." Remembering that the definition of Chicano, derived from Mexica, is one "who follows the Feathered Serpent;" metaphorically this means "one who worships the Great Spirit."

Thus is revealed the location of *Tamoanchan*: where our spirits re-integrate with the Great Spirit in preparation for the next lifetime. For Chicanos, *Tamoanchan* is the same as our spiritual Aztlan. ***Ella/El es Dios!***

2

The Red Nation pueblos of Aztlan

True to the Law of Duality, if the *spiritual Aztlan* exists, then there must be a twin to this *spiritual Aztlan*. There is. They are the Red Nation pueblos of Aztlan. These pueblos are composed of individuals, as all pueblos are, except that these pueblos exist wherever a Chicano is. They exist wherever a Chicano is, because every pueblo of Aztlan is contained within the consciousness of a Chicana/o/x. In that sense, the Red Nation pueblos of Aztlan are spiritual and physical at the same time.

The existence of these pueblos was accomplished by the spiritual declaration of Alurista at Denver in March of 1969, as noted above. He stated:

"With our hearts in our hands and our hands in the soil, we declare the independence of our Mestizo nation, a Bronze people with a Bronze culture. Before the world, before all of North America, before our brothers in the Bronze continent, we are a Nation of free pueblos, we are Aztlán."

Most analyses of Aztlan, as was discussed in section one above, have centered on the possible location of the Aztlan homeland of the Aztecs. But it is clear from a focused reading of Alurista's declaration, that he was not talking about the Aztlan of the Aztecs, but rather was giving notice of the birth of a new Nation, composed of free pueblos. This declaration was made to the whole world, and specifically to the Red Nations of Abya Yala. What is the importance for Chicanos of the existence of the mestizo Nation of Aztlan?

The saga of the mestizo in Mexican history, is that of the orphan rejected by both parents. For those mestizos seeking to honor their native roots, the declaration of a Mestizo Nation means Chicanos now have their own tent within the compound of the Red Nations. Chicanos no longer need to seek acceptance by, or accommodation with, any Red Nations pueblo, be it in Mexico or the United States. We have our own house, our own pueblos, which are Aztlan!

Note: being mestizo (mixed-blood) has less distinction within Native Americans. It is estimated that the majority of Native Americans in this country are mixed blood of varying blood quantum.

The pueblos of Aztlan thus are wherever a Chicano lives. Every Chicano barrio, every Chicano household, is a pueblo of Aztlan. We are eternal spirits experiencing a unique human lifetime, which is why we individually comprise a pueblo, and are a Nation of free pueblos/human beings/Chicanos.

There is no further definition of Alurista's declaration, and the significance of the Declaration has been overlooked in the last 50 + years. It is time for this Nation of free pueblos to be further defined. That is the challenge the spirit world gives the **chicanada**: define the Nation of Aztlan that we have gifted you!

This challenge from the spirit world means there is a lot of work that needs to be done, in arriving at an agreed definition/purpose, of the mestizo Nation of Aztlan. Hopefully the process of debate and discussion on defining the Nation of Aztlan will follow within our communities as our native identity grows. What is clear is that this Nation exists in our consciousness. It is not physical. To exist in consciousness, means the energy/Life for the Nation of Aztlan, is spiritual.

This discussion also brings up a subject regarding the health status of the Chicano Movement. Is it dead as some have declared? Nothing could be further from the truth. There are millions more Chicanos today than in the 1960's. Not only are there many more Chicanos, but today's version also is even more conciente (conscious). The Chicano Movement has just transformed with the times, as everything must, due to evolution, and continues to be expressed in multiple creative ways by the free pueblo individuals of Aztlan.

Though the expanded definition of the mestizo Nation of Aztlan is yet to come, we can ascertain numerous positive evolutions of a native consciousness within the framework of the Nation of Aztlan. Chicanos can pursue our own individual definition of what constitutes a native consciousness and apply this consciousness to travel on our own personal Red Road. We are free human beings and eternal spirits experiencing our own unique human lifetime. ***El/Ella es Dios!***

Part Five

What shall I take with me?
Will I leave nothing about me over the earth?
How shall my heart act?
Is it that we come in vain to live,
to sprout over the earth?
Let us leave at least flowers,
let us leave at least songs...

... Nezahualcóyotl
Mexica/Alcohua

1

Creating a Chicano Red Road

Leaving Christianity for the Red Road does not mean you stop believing in God. All religions/worldviews throughout the world are paths to the same and only Absolute Being. The notable exception is Buddhism, which doesn't advocate belief in "God," but whose final evolution, Nirvana, is identical to the Mexica concept of "re-integration with the Great Spirit."

I gladly exchanged the Catholic God, who had no description, other than that He was white, male, and Omnipotent, for a native Great Spirit. My names for the Absolute Being are God, Dios, Ometeotl, or Great Spirit. I am comfortable using all four names for my belief in a Dual Energy Absolute Being. Since your relationship with the Great Spirit on the Red Road is personal, my Great Spirit is a Duality of female/male, positive/negative, Energy. You alone decide the name and description of the Absolute Being.

What is different is that Jesus no longer has much relevance on the Red Road. Aside from being respected as a prophet of another religion, Jesus' relevance lies in the use of his image as a symbol. Symbolism such as the cross, which for the native is a **nahui ollin** representing the Four Directions. While prophets are not needed on the Red Road, mutual respect dictates that those prophets such as Jesus, Mohammed, the Buddha, and others, be totally respected for their contributions to mankind and Life in general.

From a native perspective, these prophets appeared the world over because the Great Spirit dictated that their wisdom and example were needed for human spiritual growth. The wisdom of the Great Spirit inspiring these prophets is manifested by the number of adherents each religion (Christianity, Islam, Buddhism) has in the world today.

Yet, the Great Spirit dictated another path for the Red Nations; a path that doesn't require prophets, churches or temples, religious orders, or the like. A personal path for every member of the Red Nations.

If leaving Christianity is too drastic for some, practicing some form of Christianity is possible while walking on the Red Road. Many of the original pueblos in Mexico have been practicing syncretic Catholicism since *la Conquista*. This is a form of Catholicism in Mexico where natives use Catholic churches, symbols, and saints, as representatives of their own native spirits, in order to walk on their version of the Red Road.

The most vivid examples of this form of hidden native worship are San Juan Chamula in Chiapas, as well as the shrine of Chalma. Unfortunately for Chicanos, such syncretic Catholicism is not practiced in the United States. But there is no reason you, as the traveler, cannot choose to create your own syncretic Catholicism, or Christianity, as you begin to walk the Red Road.

When you travel on the Red Road, the changes you make to worship the Great Spirit are made internally. There is no need to advertise or declare that you have left Christianity and are now walking the Red Road. The Red Road is personal and voluntary, it does not advertise for any new travelers. The Red Road does NOT proselytize, go door-to-door with pamphlets to convert you, or send youth on 2-year missions to "spread the word." You make the decision to travel on the Red Road for your own personal reasons.

Perhaps you want to explore the cosmic you, and why you are living a lifetime. Perhaps you want to define what your relationship is to the rest of humanity and all our relatives on Mother Earth. Perhaps you are seeking responsibility, wish to open the door to communication with the spirit world, or are ready to grasp/explore your cosmic future. A significant part of your decolonization is exactly that: to understand that you are experiencing a unique human lifetime, and you, and you alone, will live this lifetime with the identity/vision that you embrace. You need not apologize or explain your decisions to anyone.

If you are an atheist or agnostic, perhaps being exposed to the scientific foundations of the Red Road, will generate enough interest for you to explore this part of your native self. *Lo que este programado.*

2

Three Steps to Decolonization

1. Secure your identity as a Chicana/o/x. Elevate your culture to be at least equal to the gabacho's, and, for spiritual purposes, make your culture superior.

2. Deconstruct the gabacho's true history. Flush away his white supremacy worldview and spiritual poverty. Embrace true Democracy.

3. Say goodbye to the white supremacy practice of Christianity. You don't need a foreign road to reach the Great Spirit.

    We are now ready to create/build, our own personal native mestizo version of the Red Road, a Chicana/o/x Red Road. We are empowered to create our own Red Road as members of the bronze Nation of Aztlan. We are part of the Red Nations. We are free human beings with a cosmic purpose and destiny. We are eternal spirits experiencing a unique human lifetime. We are One with the Many relatives/organisms on Mother Earth.

    The following basic tenets/principles correspond to a general Red Nations worldview that can be used to walk any Red Road. Let's consider them one-by-one.

1. Open your Heart and Soul to the Great Spirit.

All Life in the Universe exists, because of, is, the Great Spirit. Honor, respect, and show your love to the Great Spirit for this blessing of Life on a daily basis.

2. The Earth is our Mother, care for Her.

The Earth is our mother because she is a living being, with her own soul and spirit. The Four elements and soul that make our bodies, all come from her. She is our provider and teacher. Maintain a clean environment and learn her lessons.

3. Honor all your Relations.

All organisms of Life on Mother Earth are parts of her. Thus, recognize all organisms as our relatives. All organisms/forms have their own souls and spirits.

4. All Life is Sacred. Treat all Beings with Respect.

There is no organism too small or repulsive that isn't a form of the Great Spirit and the sacred Diversity of Life. Humans are not superior to any other organism. We have the responsibility to maintain the harmony with all our relations.

5. Take from the Earth what is Needed and Nothing More.

Mother Earth is not for sale. Honor the natural laws and take only what you need with respect. We live in a reciprocal world with all other organisms. Seek balance in everything.

6. Do what Needs to be Done for the Good of the All.
Always consider your actions and how they will impact others before you act. Consider the group, not only yourself. All Life is connected.

7. Speak the Truth and maintain Honesty.
Avoid gossip and telling lies. These negative activities disrupt the harmony you are seeking, and need, to walk the Red Road. Always energize the atoms in the air with the truth.

8. Take Responsibility for your Actions.
Stop blaming others for your actions. You alone are responsible for the decisions/choices you make. Your actions are part of the interactive relationship you have with the Great Spirit.

****

These basic tenets are the foundation for any Red Road. Incorporate them into your vision of Reality and Life and began the process of creating your own Chicano/a/x Red Road. Implement MEN by Believing in your Road, then Create the description of your Road, and then Do, by traveling on your Road. The heavy lifting from this point on, depends totally on your efforts, or not.

C/S

www.ingramcontent.com/pod-product-compliance
Lightning Source LLC
Chambersburg PA
CBHW020906080526
44589CB00011B/465